# Puzzles

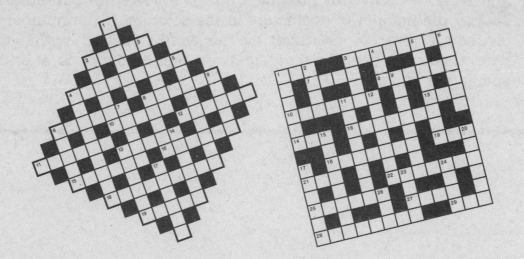

# Publisher's Note:

**E**ACH CROSSWORD PUZZLE CLUE is followed in parentheses by the number of characters in the solution. If the number of characters given is preceded by the word "British" within the parentheses, it denotes that the word being sought is a Britsh spelling or idiom.

# BIG BIG BOOK OF Crosswords

**Can your brain handle the strain?**

## Puzzles to get you thinking . . .

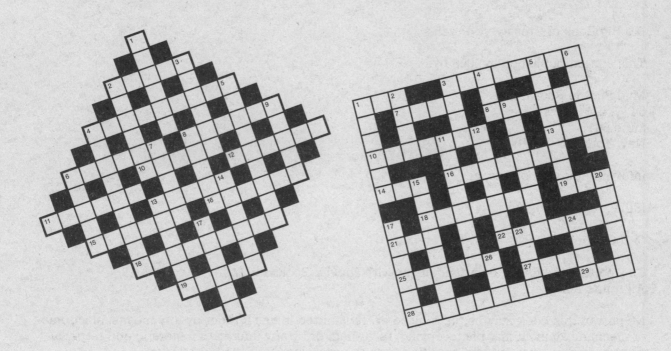

MUD PUDDLE BOOKS, INC.
New York, New York

Big Big Book of Crossword Puzzles

This edition published in 2005 by:

Mud Puddle Books, Inc.
54 W. 21st Street
Suite 601
New York, NY 10010

info@mudpuddlebooks.com

ISBN: 1-59412-069-2

Cover designed by Alan Carr

Printed in the United States of America

# Puzzle 1

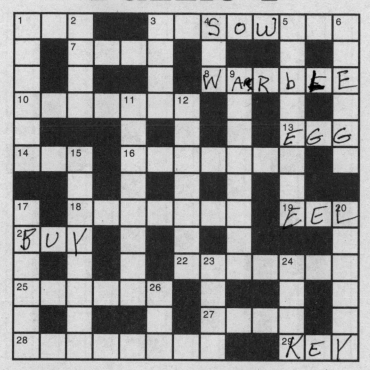

## Across

**1.** Tear (3)
**3.** Waver (8)
**7.** Monster (4)
**8.** Trill (6)
**10.** Reflexive pronoun (7)
**13.** Ovum (3)
**14.** Quarrel (3)
**16.** Citadel (7)
**18.** Bridge (7)
**19.** Slippery fish (3)
**21.** Be in debt (3)
**22.** Someone who breaks free (7)
**25.** Show off (6)
**27.** Affirm (4)
**28.** Jeopardize (8)
**29.** It unlocks a lock (3)

## Down

**1.** Somewhat (6)
**2.** Verse form (4)
**3.** Cure (4)
**4.** Adult female hog (3)
**5.** The atmosphere of an environment (8)
**6.** Come forth (6)
**9.** Aesthetic (8)
**11.** Decorate with heraldic arms (8)
**12.** Crevice (7)
**15.** Radio frequency (8)
**17.** Popular drink (6)
**20.** Margin (6)
**23.** Heavenly body (4)
**24.** Meat from a pig (4)
**26.** Label (3)

**solution on page 170**

# Puzzle 2

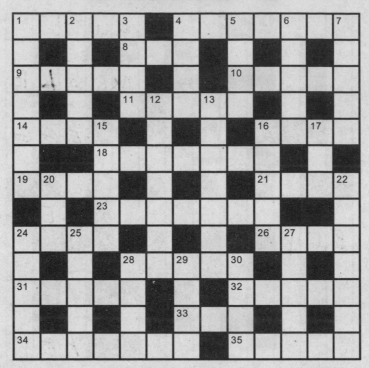

# Across

1. Inundated (5)
4. Inanely foolish (7)
8. Important timber or shade tree (3)
9. Empty area (5)
10. Colorless gas (5)
11. Compare (5)
14. Stare at lustfully (4)
16. Fluid-filled sac (4)
18. Nazi secret police force (7)
19. Antlered animal (4)
21. Impact (as from a collision) (4)
23. Voter (7)
24. Religious fanatic group (4)
26. Domed recess (4)
28. Glued (5)
31. Existing (5)
32. Result (5)
33. Nocturnal bird of prey (3)
34. Leather from the swine (7)
35. Tartan (5)

# Down

1. Run away (7)
2. Make use of (5)
3. Back part of a shoe (4)
4. In a murderous frenzy (4)
5. Graphic symbol (4)
6. Elephant tusk (5)
7. Construct a building (5)
12. Scrutinize (7)
13. Stretchy fabric (7)
15. Heron (5)
16. Venomous snake (5)
17. Quantity obtained by addition (3)
20. Flightless bird (3)
22. Make believe (7)
24. Spasm (5)
25. Telling fibs (5)
27. Shaped and dried dough (5)
28. Look for (4)
29. Atop (4)
30. Large brown seaweed (4)

solution on page 170

# Puzzle 3

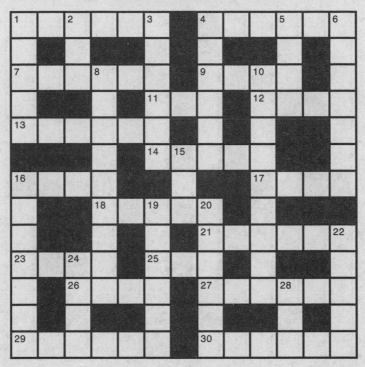

## Across

1. Wicked, unholy (6)
4. Zodiacal sign (6)
7. Solid lump of a precious metal (6)
9. Contest of speed (4)
11. Adult female bird (3)
12. Crippled (4)
13. Rhododendron-like shrub (6)
14. Backslide (5)
16. Heroic tale (4)
17. Necessity (4)
18. Period of darkness (5)
21. Schedule (6)
23. Promises (4)
25. Standard strokes made for a hole in golf (3)
26. Slippery fish (4)
27. Lubricating substance (6)
29. Think highly of (6)
30. Natural endowment (6)

## Down

1. Father Christmas (5)
2. Over-worked horse (3)
3. Deadly (6)
4. Widely cultivated vegetable (6)
5. Fast-running and flightless South American bird (4)
6. Cut off from a whole (7)
8. Stimulate, into action (British, 9)
10. Customers (9)
15. Deciduous tree (3)
16. Save from ruin or destruction (7)
19. Common white or colorless mineral (6)
20. Objective (6)
22. Proficient (5)
24. Shed tears (4)
28. Bladed, chopping tool (3)

# Puzzle 4

## Across

1. Typical dwelling-place (5)
3. It is seen as a narrow waxing crescent (3,4)
6. The act of coming together again (7)
8. Farewell (5)
10. Large back molars (6,5)
12. Verruca, for example (4)
13. Craftily (5)
15. Single article (4)
17. Form into one cluster (11)
19. Harden (5)
20. Glands near to the kidneys (7)
21. Jellied sweet (7)
22. Frequently (5)

## Down

1. Cultivating tool (6)
2. Brightly shining (6)
3. Religious woman (3)
4. Gnat (5)
5. Zero (6)
7. Former sweetheart (3,5)
9. Begged (8)
10. Incorrect (5)
11. Select group (5)
14. Surface of a walkway (6)
15. Reflexive pronoun (6)
16. Plain-woven cotton fabric (6)
18. Glaringly vivid (5)
20. Viper (3)

solution on page 171

# Puzzle 5

## Across

**1.** Adhered (5)
**3.** Rainy season (7)
**6.** Submit or live through (7)
**8.** Spy (5)
**10.** The legal lowest remuneration (7,4)
**12.** Nautical mile (4)
**13.** Donated (5)
**15.** At the summit of (4)
**17.** A dispute where there is strong disagreement (11)
**19.** Exactly matched (5)
**20.** Feminine (7)
**21.** Bloated (7)
**22.** Senior (5)

## Down

**1.** Make a noise like a parrot (6)
**2.** Approval (6)
**3.** The sound made by a cow (3)
**4.** Tendon connecting muscle to bone (5)
**5.** Son of one's brother or sister (6)
**7.** American football field (8)
**9.** Conscience (5-3)
**10.** Grieve (5)
**11.** Cordiality (5)
**14.** Admittance (6)
**15.** Launch an attack or assault on (6)
**16.** Orison (6)
**18.** Hang back (5)
**20.** Pallid (3)

solution on page 171

# Puzzle 6

## Across

**1.** Partially melted snow (5)

**3.** Being in charge of (7)

**6.** Raise in value or esteem (7)

**8.** Sharp (5)

**10.** Not mentally confused (5-6)

**12.** Child's toy (4)

**13.** Glossy (5)

**15.** Sudden attack (4)

**17.** Pigeonholed (11)

**19.** Holy book (5)

**20.** A special anniversary (7)

**21.** Toothed wheel engaged with a pawl (7)

**22.** Deserve, earn (5)

## Down

**1.** Without much intelligence (6)

**2.** A document that can be rolled up (6)

**3.** Prevarication (3)

**4.** Russian country house (5)

**5.** Avaricious (6)

**7.** Part of a prison for condemned inmates (5,3)

**9.** Expression of gratitude (5,3)

**10.** Near (5)

**11.** Fearful expectation (5)

**14.** Line on a weather map (6)

**15.** Elaborate (6)

**16.** Fraudulence (6)

**18.** An object that has survived from the past (5)

**20.** Write briefly or hurriedly (3)

# Puzzle 7

## Across

1. Have the financial means to buy something (6)
4. Relating to or using sight (6)
8. French term meaning farewell (5)
9. Thin slice of toast with savory food (6)
10. Unclothed (5)
12. Merry-go-round (8)
13. Institute legal proceedings against (3)
14. Came first (3)
15. Dried hulled vegetable; used in soup (5-3)
18. Boredom (5)
19. Corresponding exactly (6)
20. Fish with a hook (5)
21. The season including Christmas (6)
22. Lucky charm (6)

## Down

1. By surprise (5)
2. Enclosed heat-producing chamber (7)
3. Dandy (4)
5. Bedspread (11)
6. Landscaped area for playing golf (5)
7. A concluding summary (7)
8. Suitable and fitting (11)
11. Game bird (5)
13. By unspecified means (7)
14. Sing carols (7)
16. Aromatic, edible bulb (5)
17. Dark (5)
19. Arm bone (4)

# Puzzle 8

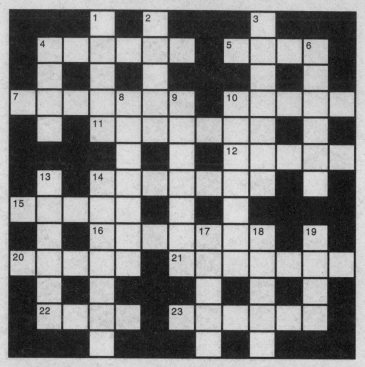

## Across

4. Browned (6)
5. Eye sore (4)
7. Eradicate (7)
10. Distance downwards (5)
11. A fever (7)
12. Pamphlet (5)
14. Re-establish (2-5)
15. Conducting stick (5)
16. Outlet of river to sea (7)
20. Forest clearing (5)
21. Cocktail (7)
22. Close by (4)
23. Sentimental (6)

## Down

1. Leg joint (5)
2. Lavish meal (5)
3. Dutch province (7)
4. Cylindrical container (4)
6. One or other (6)
8. Infuriate (7)
9. Dreadful (7)
10. Throw out (7)
13. Type of coat (6)
14. English girls' school (7)
17. Church passage (5)
18. Raising agent (5)
19. Infant (4)

solution on page 172

# Puzzle 9

## Across

1. Scottish landowner (5)
4. Polar feature (3-3)
9. Weighting for ship (7)
10. Meat from stomach (5)
11. Unfasten (4)
12. English novelist (7)
13. Female deer (3)
14. Was certain (4)
16. Herb (4)
18. Globe (3)
20. Warped (7)
21. Seat (4)
24. For all (music) (5)
25. The Greek name for Odysseus (7)
26. Deepen (6)
27. Additional (5)

## Down

1. Hard work (British, 6)
2. Loafed (5)
3. Costly (4)
5. Underground cemetery (8)
6. 1853–56 war (7)
7. Gladden (6)
8. Musical study (5)
13. Residence (8)
15. Piece of material worn (mostly by men) under a collar (7)
17. Died down (6)
18. Hatred (5)
19. Sickness (6)
22. Beginning (5)
23. Cattle shed (4)

solution on page 172

# Puzzle 10

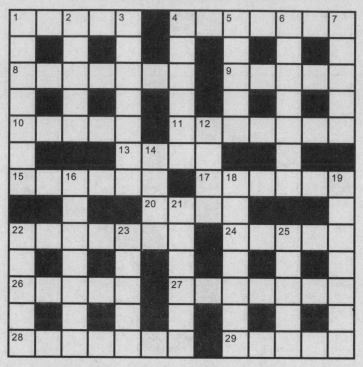

## Across

1. Unbeliever (5)
4. English king, nicknamed The Lionheart (7)
8. Muffling (7)
9. Domain (5)
10. Surpass (5)
11. Stick fruit (7)
13. Asked (4)
15. Fine white clay (6)
17. Appalled (6)
20. Ebb and flow of the sea (4)
22. Deviate (7)
24. Pertaining to the nose (5)
26. Passenger ship (5)
27. Overhead transport (7)
28. Liquor (7)
29. Confectionery (5)

## Down

1. Detachable security device (7)
2. Scale (5)
3. Kenyan capital (7)
4. Observe (6)
5. Greek island (5)
6. US state (7)
7. Disband (5)
12. Top (4)
14. Social insects (4)
16. Derived from living matter (7)
18. Of a class (7)
19. Russian novelist (7)
21. Country which shares a border with Egypt (6)
22. River-mouth (5)
23. Home planet (5)
25. Offspring (5)

solution on page 173

# Puzzle 11

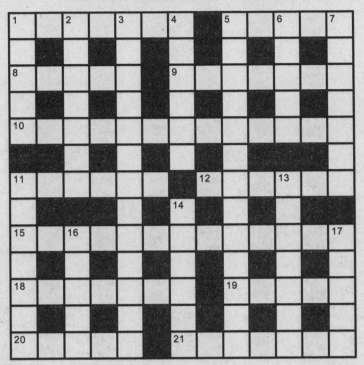

## Across

**1.** Small, flat, sweet cake (7)
**5.** Punctuation mark (5)
**8.** Burn with steam (5)
**9.** Bitterness (7)
**10.** Opposition between two conflicting ideas (13)
**11.** Buccaneer (6)
**12.** Crude (6)
**15.** Microscopic, immeasurably small (13)
**18.** Fowl that frequents coastal waters (7)
**19.** Heron (5)
**20.** Branchlet (5)
**21.** Lewd (7)

## Down

**1.** Primary (5)
**2.** Detection device (7)
**3.** Realizing (13)
**4.** Violent denunciation (6)
**5.** Awareness (13)
**6.** Native New Zealander (5)
**7.** Put into a proper or systematic order (7)
**11.** Christian clergymen (7)
**13.** Compunction (7)
**14.** Place for the teaching or practice of an art (6)
**16.** Style (5)
**17.** Metric measurement (British, 5)

solution on page 173

# Puzzle 12

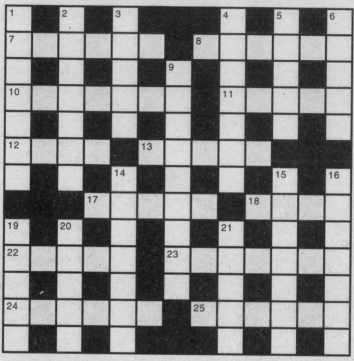

## Across

**7.** Thin slice (6)
**8.** Unsullied (6)
**10.** Welsh castle (7)
**11.** Fresh-water fish (5)
**12.** Plunder (4)
**13.** Arm-joint (5)
**17.** Refuse to go on (5)
**18.** Animal's home (4)
**22.** Noisy altercation (5)
**23.** Roman native (7)
**24.** Writer (6)
**25.** Droop (6)

## Down

**1.** Bituminous substance (7)
**2.** White-faced clown (7)
**3.** Irritated (5)
**4.** Cigar (7)
**5.** Academy Award (5)
**6.** Indian city (5)
**9.** Painful swelling on hand or foot, in cold weather (9)
**14.** Inflatable bag (7)
**15.** Tiredness (7)
**16.** Large packet of shares (7)
**19.** Submarine (1-4)
**20.** Coat in fat (5)
**21.** Tree from which a sugary syrup is produced (5)

solution on page 173

# Puzzle 13

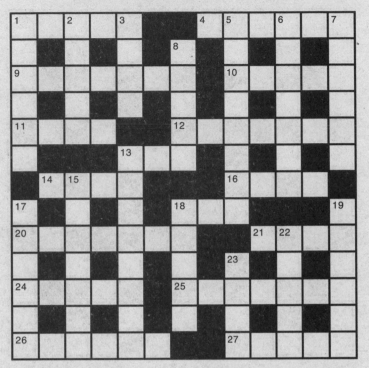

## Across

1. Ballroom dance (5)
4. Pester (6)
9. End of marriage (7)
10. Banter (5)
11. Skulk (4)
12. Ore (7)
13. Vital (3)
14. Smoke-duct (4)
16. Short note (4)
18. Eyelid swelling (3)
20. Poisonous weed (7)
21. Join metal (4)
24. Give speech (5)
25. Flat area in series of slopes (7)
26. Worn away (6)
27. Bring into play (5)

## Down

1. Walk like a duck (6)
2. Beau (5)
3. Nought (4)
6. Self-government (8)
6. Word of transposed letters (7)
7. Purloins (6)
8. Burglar's crowbar (5)
13. Paraffin oil (8)
15. Backache (7)
17. Silvery metal (6)
18. Flatfish (5)
19. Coming (6)
22. Make ecstatically happy (5)
23. Encourage (4)

# Puzzle 14

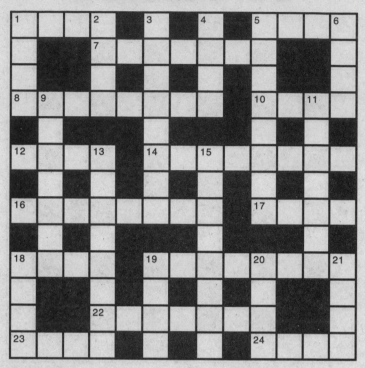

## Across

1. Small branch (4)
5. Stopper (4)
7. In poetic style (7)
8. Adolescent (8)
10. Ballet dancer's skirt (4)
12. Elderly (4)
14. Mischievous adventure (8)
16. Doubter (8)
17. Exchange (4)
18. Poems (4)
19. One who hopes for the best (8)
22. Plaintive poet (7)
23. Small cut (4)
24. Hamstring (4)

## Down

1. Bitter sweet (4)
2. Scottish valley (4)
3. Small piece (8)
4. Blemish (4)
5. Egg-laying, Australian creature (8)
6. Eastern teacher (4)
9. Given a job (7)
11. Boring (7)
13. Thick slice of bread (8)
15. Mixed drink (8)
18. Musical work (4)
19. Stove (4)
20. Flying insect (4)
21. Duty (4)

          solution on page 174

# Puzzle 15

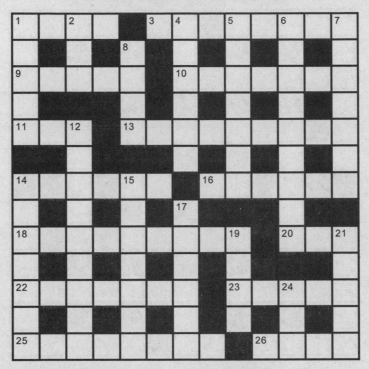

## Across

**1.** Blemish (4)
**3.** Tilted (8)
**9.** Furze (5)
**10.** Neptune's spear (7)
**11.** Lick up (3)
**13.** Emotionally shocking (9)
**14.** Customer (6)
**16.** Emergency (6)
**18.** Part of three-piece suit (9)
**20.** Prosecute (3)
**22.** Calamitous (7)
**23.** Become invalid through time (5)
**25.** Spotted (8)
**26.** Method used to achieve a particular result, especially in a game (4)

## Down

**1.** Ring-shaped bread roll (5)
**2.** Paddle (3)
**4.** Bandit (6)
**5.** Water sportsman (7)
**6.** Two singers (9)
**7.** Finds (7)
**8.** Air-hole (4)
**12.** Rudimentary (9)
**14.** Definitely not heroes (7)
**15.** Mesh (7)
**17.** Creamy dish (6)
**19.** Charge (4)
**21.** Foe (5)
**24.** Mate (3)

# Puzzle 16

## Across

**1.** Digging implement (5)

**3.** Sensationalist journalism (7)

**6.** Artist's paint-mixing board (7)

**8.** An advantageous purchase (5)

**10.** Being everywhere at once (11)

**12.** Following (4)

**13.** Neuters (animal) (5)

**15.** Cream off (4)

**17.** Suitable and fitting (11)

**19.** Move smoothly along a surface (5)

**20.** Noisy talk (7)

**21.** Spring back (7)

**22.** Large body of water (5)

## Down

**1.** Draw off liquid by atmospheric pressure (6)

**2.** Indulged in a fantasy (6)

**3.** Golf peg (3)

**4.** Asian water lily (5)

**5.** Become wider (6)

**7.** Car exhaust (8)

**9.** Warm-water lobsters without claws (8)

**10.** Eurasian primrose with yellow flowers (5)

**11.** Call to mind (5)

**14.** Type of salad (6)

**15.** Motionless (6)

**16.** Head nurse (6)

**18.** Exhibition of cowboy skills (5)

**20.** Rechewed food (3)

solution on page 175

# Puzzle 17

## Across

1. Infertile (6)
4. Save from sin (6)
8. Bird's home (4)
10. Crunchy, green salad vegetable (8)
12. Grace, style (8)
13. Couch (4)
14. Spoil (3)
15. Dictatorship (7)
17. Globe (3)
19. Particle (4)
21. Eavesdrop (8)
22. Aromatic (8)
24. A friendly nation (4)
26. Walk ostentatiously (6)
27. Type of monkey, macaque (6)

## Down

1. Small rounded cake, often toasted (3)
2. Withdraw (7)
3. Cleared of weapons such as H-bombs, etc (7,4)
5. Large Australian bird (3)
6. Special design or symbol (6)
7. Pungent leaves used as seasoning (8)
9. EC monetary unit (4)
11. Communication sent successively to many people (5,6)
13. White, early spring flower (8)
16. Distance measured in three-foot units (7)
18. Boundary line (6)
20. Egg-shaped (4)
23. Saucepan cover (3)
25. Affirmative answer (3)

solution on page 175

# Puzzle 18

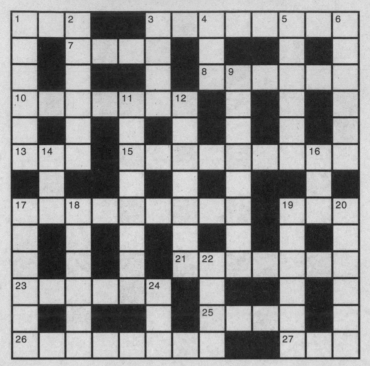

## Across

1. Add together (3)
3. Hussy, loose woman (8)
7. Fiend (4)
8. Author (6)
10. Creation of the highest excellence (7)
13. Implement used to propel or steer a boat (3)
15. Cloth used to cover the eyes (9)
17. Ad lib (9)
19. Small drink (3)
21. Squeeze out (7)
23. Venue (6)
25. Excitedly eager (4)
26. Chinese meat or fish dish, stir-fried with vegetables (4,4)
27. Sense organ (3)

## Down

1. Ornamental plaster used to cover walls (6)
2. Angora yarn (6)
3. One of the two competitions in the next to last round of an elimination tournament (4)
4. Uncooked (3)
5. Vegetable (6)
6. Sluggish (6)
9. Set again after an initial failure (8)
11. Part of a calculation (8)
12. Deprive of the use of a limb (7)
14. Direct (3)
16. Ornamental garland (3)
17. Slanted lettering (6)
18. Blanket-like cloak (6)
19. Blur (6)
20. Favor (6)
22. Medical 'photograph' (1-3)
24. Former French coin (3)

solution on page 175

# Puzzle 19

## Across

1. Make steady (6)
4. Sounded one's opinion (6)
8. Overabundance (4)
10. Flowering vine (8)
12. Not fully developed (8)
14. The French word for Christmas (4)
15. Male offspring (3)
16. Lackadaisical (7)
18. Indian island (3)
20. Equips (4)
22. Friend lodging with you (4-4)
23. Squealer (8)
26. Heroic tale (4)
28. A formal expression of praise (6)
29. Conventional (6)

## Down

1. Large (3)
2. Mound made by social insects (7)
3. Cut the grass (3)
5. Choose or show a preference (3)
6. Slices meat joint (6)
7. Blind alleys (4,4)
9. Swimming pool (4)
11. Variety of mandarin orange (7)
13. Lower limit (7)
14. A reply of denial (8)
17. Chest of drawers (7)
19. Giving a false appearance of frankness (6)
21. An association of criminals (4)
24. Small carpet (3)
25. An unbroken series of events (3)
27. A pointed tool (3)

solution on page 176

# Puzzle 20

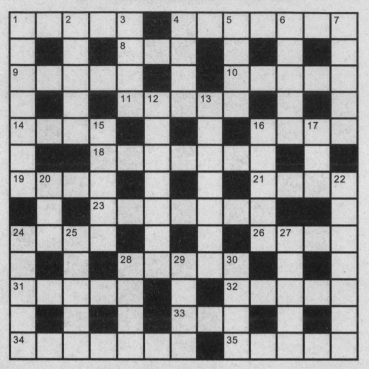

## Across

1. A secret store of valuables (5)
4. Ornamental cloth pad worn on the shoulder (7)
8. Unwell (3)
9. Worthy (5)
10. Hand tool for boring holes (5)
11. Adult male singing voice (5)
14. Explosive device (4)
16. Smooth-tongued (4)
18. Excel or defeat in a game (7)
19. Soft light (4)
21. A secret look (4)
23. Pencil rubbers (7)
24. Rear of an aircraft (4)
26. Yesteryear (4)
28. Fashion (5)
31. Fool (5)
32. Cherished desire (5)
33. Fall behind (3)
34. Jellied sweet (7)
35. Bread-raising agent (5)

## Down

1. Container for small personal items (7)
2. Photo book (5)
3. Prescribed selection of foods (4)
4. Panache (4)
5. Distant (4)
6. Legitimate (5)
7. Pulsate (5)
12. Participant in some activity (7)
13. Mineral source (3,4)
15. Intestine (5)
16. Romany (5)
17. Frozen water (3)
20. Grazing land (3)
22. Acquire as first-comer (3-4)
24. Attaching (5)
25. Dialect (5)
27. Musical drama (5)
28. Agitate (4)
29. Bark in a high-pitched tone (4)
30. Highly-strung (4)

solution on page 176

# Puzzle 21

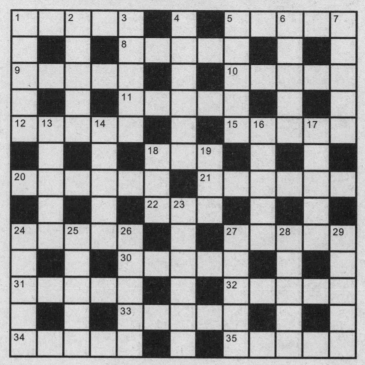

## Across

**1.** Mountaineering spike (5)
**5.** Stop from happening (5)
**8.** Accepted practice (5)
**9.** Smallest amount (5)
**10.** Habituate (5)
**11.** Object (5)
**12.** Avail oneself to (5)
**15.** Improve (5)
**18.** Show displeasure vocally (3)
**20.** Administrative unit of government (6)
**21.** Form of communication (6)
**22.** Demented (3)
**24.** Sound off (5)
**27.** Banquet (5)
**30.** Monarch (5)
**31.** Laundering appliance that removes moisture (5)
**32.** Young night-bird (5)
**33.** Open (5)
**34.** Revolving arm of a distributor (5)
**35.** Speed (5)

## Down

**1.** Bohemian dance (5)
**2.** Hobo (5)
**3.** Bonkers (5)
**4.** Type of cloth (6)
**5.** Ecru (5)
**6.** Reproductive structure (5)
**7.** Work dough (5)
**13.** Chubby (5)
**14.** A long stay in bed in the morning (3-2)
**16.** Unit of length (British, 5)
**17.** Demands (5)
**18.** A disreputable wanderer (3)
**19.** Elderly (3)
**23.** Slumbering (6)
**24.** Command (5)
**25.** Imbecile (5)
**26.** Mistake (5)
**27.** A mass of small bubbles (5)
**28.** Book of maps (5)
**29.** Levy of one tenth of something (5)

**solution on page 176**

# Puzzle 22

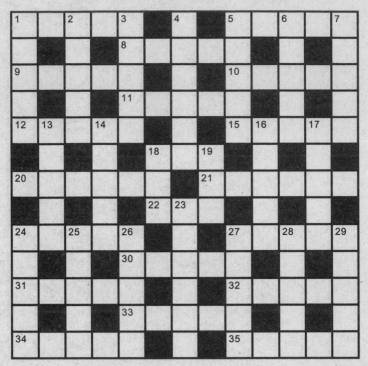

## Across

1. Loft (5)
5. Bring upon oneself (5)
8. Circular (5)
9. Saturate (5)
10. Electronic message (1-4)
11. Italian thin bread dough with topping (5)
12. Employment (5)
15. Exalted (5)
18. Do needlework (3)
20. Treeless, Arctic plain (6)
21. Evade (6)
22. Bounder (3)
24. The sepals of a flower (5)
27. Fad (5)
30. Third planet from the Sun (5)
31. Quantity of twelve items (5)
32. Data entered on computer (5)
33. Projecting bay window (5)
34. Thick sap from tree (5)
35. Gangly (5)

## Down

1. Au revoir (5)
2. Shinbone (5)
3. Thin pancake (5)
4. Drink greedily (6)
5. Perfect (5)
6. Husk (5)
7. Marked recovery of strength (5)
13. Aqualung (5)
14. Divine (5)
16. Annual film industry award (5)
17. A yellow quartz (5)
18. Pouch (3)
19. Marry (3)
23. Frightened (6)
24. Durable aromatic wood (5)
25. Stagnates (5)
26. Inert gas (5)
27. Cool down (5)
28. Poplar tree (5)
29. Way in (5)

solution on page 177

# Puzzle 23

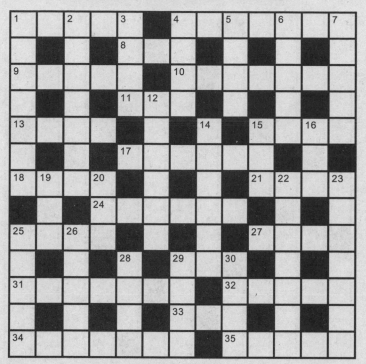

## Across

**1.** In the center of (5)
**4.** Band of flowers (7)
**8.** Snake-like fish (3)
**9.** Tool used for drawing lines (5)
**10.** Radioactive metallic element (7)
**11.** Encountered (3)
**13.** Blotted (4)
**15.** A stand to support a coffin (4)
**17.** Brass resembling gold; used to decorate furniture (6)
**18.** Male sovereign (4)
**21.** Control on a radio (4)
**24.** Maintenance (6)
**25.** Give sanction to (4)
**27.** Municipality smaller than a city (4)
**29.** In favor of (3)
**31.** Principal theme in a speech (7)
**32.** Effigy (5)
**33.** Imp (3)
**34.** Beaver-like aquatic rodent (7)
**35.** Upright (5)

## Down

**1.** Experiencing motion nausea (7)
**2.** Waterproof raincoat (7)
**3.** Minute life-form (4)
**4.** Surfeit (4)
**5.** Horse coloring (4)
**6.** Excuse (5)
**7.** Take exception to (5)
**12.** Word uttered by Archimedes (6)
**14.** A short jacket (6)
**15.** Partially opened flower (3)
**16.** Division of geological time (3)
**19.** Kind (3)
**20.** Rope used to brace a tent (3)
**22.** Set apart (7)
**23.** Lax (7)
**25.** Fiber obtained by unraveling old rope (5)
**26.** Bottomless gulf or pit (5)
**28.** Room access (4)
**29.** Imperial units of length (4)
**30.** Overabundant (4)

solution on page 177

# Puzzle 24

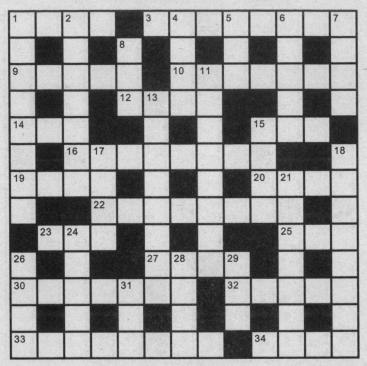

## Across

1. The cards held in a card game (4)
3. Duplicate or match (8)
9. Thoroughly unpleasant (5)
10. Casual tops (1-6)
12. Long narrative poem (4)
14. Adult male swan (3)
15. Organ of sight (3)
16. Characteristic of former times (3,5)
19. Cunning (4)
20. No longer retained (4)
22. Breathed (8)
23. Consumed (3)
25. Twosome (3)
27. Squeal of a pig (4)
30. Secret police force used by the Nazis in World War II (7)
32. Generally incompetent (5)
33. Ultimately following (8)
34. Adult male horse kept for breeding (4)

## Down

1. Manacle (8)
2. Safe place to hatch eggs (7)
4. Not in favor of (4)
5. Burnt remains (3)
6. Large truck (5)
7. Deprivation (4)
8. Colorant (3)
11. Type of arachnid, with a sting in the tail (8)
13. Loan office (8)
15. Boundary (4)
17. Ancient Greek harp (4)
18. Infatuated (8)
21. Scrap of fabric (7)
24. A sense of good style! (5)
26. Monster (4)
28. A tiny amount (4)
29. Family (3)
31. Astern (3)

solution on page 177

# Puzzle 25

## Across

1. Herbivorous land turtle (8)
5. An association of criminals (4)
9. Swivel (5)
10. Involvement (7)
11. Small recess opening off a larger room (6)
12. Boredom (5)
14. Audition (3,3)
16. Heat (6)
19. Brand name (5)
21. Go up (6)
24. Protective shoe-coverings (7)
25. Spooky (5)
26. Cloth covering to keep a teapot warm (4)
27. Informal photograph (8)

## Down

1. Of the highest quality (4)
2. Competition (7)
3. Get the better of (5)
4. Short temper (6)
6. Fire-raising (5)
7. Shoot-out (8)
8. Photographic equipment (6)
13. Vigorously active (8)
15. Set down cargo (6)
17. Sovereign (7)
18. Sweet, dark purple plum (6)
20. Consecrate (5)
22. Weak cry of a young bird (5)
23. Chair (4)

**solution on page 178**

# Puzzle 26

## Across

**1.** One-hundredth of the value of a dollar (4)
**3.** It's hung up for Santa (8)
**9.** Solemn (7)
**10.** Drug addicts (slang) (5)
**11.** Front of a jersey, cut to a point (1-4)
**12.** Come into possession of (6)
**14.** Red-haired (6)
**16.** Disease of the skin (6)
**19.** Allot (6)
**21.** Decree (5)
**24.** Wicker basket used to hold fish (5)
**25.** Machine that processes materials by crushing (7)
**26.** Characteristic of a particular area (8)
**27.** Simple (4)

## Down

**1.** A split (8)
**2.** Hospital worker (5)
**4.** Indelible design on the skin (6)
**5.** Make amorous advances towards (5)
**6.** Make a list of (7)
**7.** A sudden rapid flow (4)
**8.** Challenge aggressively (6)
**13.** Revealing supreme skill (8)
**15.** Fund of money put by as a reserve (4,3)
**17.** Churchman (6)
**18.** Brain-teaser (6)
**20.** Hut made of compacted snow (5)
**22.** Asian country (5)
**23.** Mark of wound (4)

solution on page 178

# Puzzle 27

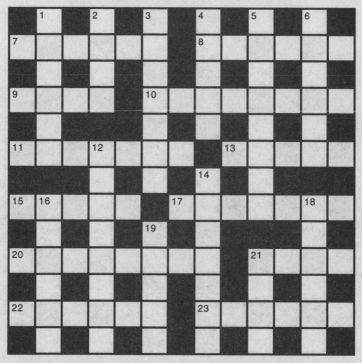

## Across

7. Severity (British, 6)
8. Far from the intended target (6)
9. Piece of music (4)
10. Teach (8)
11. Soft indoor shoe (7)
13. Facial hair (5)
15. Wrath (5)
17. Dirigible (7)
20. A cutting implement (8)
21. Roman cloak (4)
22. Tunnels occupied by rabbits (6)
23. Condone (6)

## Down

1. Chase away (6)
2. Flip a coin (4)
3. Short preview of a film or TV program (7)
4. Oversight (5)
5. First courses (8)
6. Zodiacal constellation (6)
12. Insistence (8)
14. Paper hankies (7)
16. Liquid produced by a flower (6)
18. Consume, absorb (6)
19. Discovered (5)
21. Equipment for a horse (4)

# Puzzle 28

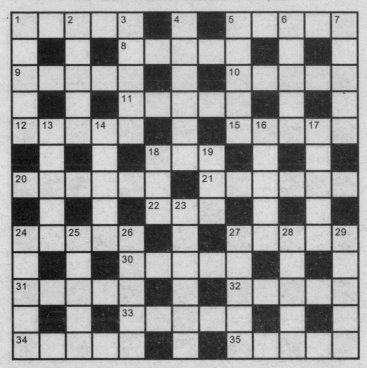

## Across

1. Lucifer (5)
5. Intermission (5)
8. Wipe off (5)
9. Loop formed in a cord or rope (5)
10. Self-justification (5)
11. Put off (5)
12. Rile (5)
15. Long pointed weapon (5)
18. Ancient (3)
20. Be present at (6)
21. Capital of Saudi Arabia (6)
22. Period in time (3)
24. Principal (5)
27. Rulers of Russia (5)
30. Large artery (5)
31. Kingdom (5)
32. Feeling of personal worth (5)
33. Leave or strike out, as of vowels (5)
34. Improve (5)
35. Piece of poetry (5)

## Down

1. Father Christmas (5)
2. Prickle (5)
3. Destitute (5)
4. Licit (6)
5. Milky-white gem (5)
6. Coupling (5)
7. Select group (5)
13. Nick (5)
14. Abnormally fat (5)
16. Bottomless gulf or pit (5)
17. Drink made from apple juice (5)
18. Peculiar (3)
19. Remove the moisture from (3)
23. Filled with fear or apprehension (6)
24. Engrave (5)
25. Showing extreme anger (5)
26. Illustrious (5)
27. Very thin candle (5)
28. Cordiality (5)
29. Military blockade (5)

solution on page 179

# Puzzle 29

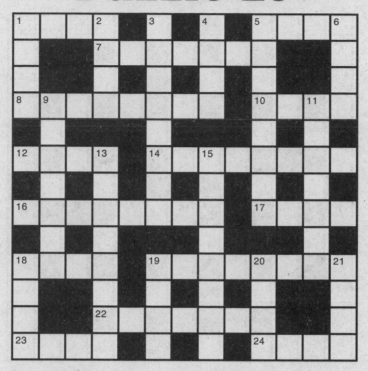

## Across

1. Canine cry (4)
5. Commotion (4)
7. Famous American waterfalls (7)
8. Oratory (8)
10. Powdery dirt (4)
12. Matured (4)
14. Disordered (8)
16. Vaulting game (4-4)
17. Pledge (4)
18. Scoff (4)
19. Tree (8)
22. South American country (7)
23. Pool of money (4)
24. Ancient city (4)

## Down

1. Male pig (4)
2. Entanglement (4)
3. Sporting dog (8)
4. Bath powder (4)
5. Spanish dance (8)
6. Filter (4)
9. Cleanliness (7)
11. Place of refuge (7)
13. Expelled from country (8)
15. Murder of a king (8)
18. Instant (colloq) (4)
19. Butt-end (4)
20. Market (4)
21. Grudging feeling (4)

solution on page 179

# Puzzle 30

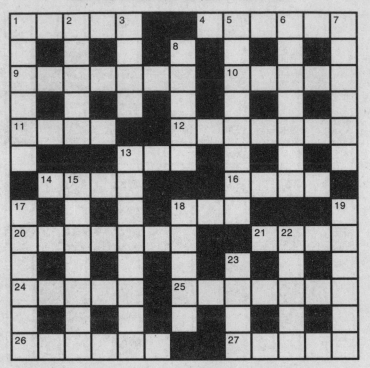

## Across

1. Wooden shoe (5)
4. Grassland (6)
9. Brochure (7)
10. Norwegian dramatist (5)
11. Went on horseback (4)
12. Dress (7)
13. Vehicle for Noah (3)
14. Celestial body (4)
16. Charge (4)
18. Youth (3)
20. Soluble case of gelatin (7)
21. Harmful (4)
24. Designation (5)
25. Italian port (7)
26. Mistakes (6)
27. Motif (5)

## Down

1. Income (6)
2. Insipid (5)
3. Ring slowly (4)
5. Diplomatic messenger (8)
6. Nauseate (7)
7. Cold season (6)
8. Twig (5)
13. Disagreement (8)
15. Betting adviser (7)
17. Mowing tool (6)
18. Animal (5)
19. Niche (6)
22. Gusto (5)
23. Blemish (4)

solution on page 179

# Puzzle 31

## Across

1. Empty (6)
4. Disastrous (5)
8. Prod (5)
9. Emit heat (7)
10. Amused (7)
11. English painter (4)
12. Period of time (3)
14. Scottish valley (4)
15. Foundation (4)
18. Joke (3)
21. Uproar (4)
23. Encased lamp (7)
25. Format (7)
26. English racecourse (5)
27. Gruesome (5)
28. Obtuse (6)

## Down

1. Ostentation (6)
2. Addition to will (7)
3. Irritating (8)
4. Lose color (4)
5. Vagabond (5)
6. German songs (6)
7. Groom's partner (5)
13. Plentiful (8)
16. Design device (7)
17. Drive from behind (6)
19. Secreting organ in animals (5)
20. Combined (6)
22. Aquatic creature (5)
24. Sell (4)

**solution on page 180**

# Puzzle 32

## Across

7. Hallowed (6)
8. European language (6)
10. Polish to high sheen (7)
11. Body part below the ribs (5)
12. Marsh plant (4)
13. Cape (5)
17. Leg joints (5)
18. Couple (4)
22. Slaver (5)
23. Cut off sun's light (7)
24. Elaborately adorned (6)
25. Three-dimensional (6)

## Down

1. Lines on weather charts (7)
2. Bright red (7)
3. Arabian goblin (5)
4. Jemmy (7)
5. Set free (5)
6. Waterfall slide (5)
9. Protected (9)
14. Blow up (7)
15. Aperitif, often served with soda (7)
16. Liberty (7)
19. Form of speech (5)
20. Indicate (5)
21. Air attack (5)

**solution on page 180**

# Puzzle 33

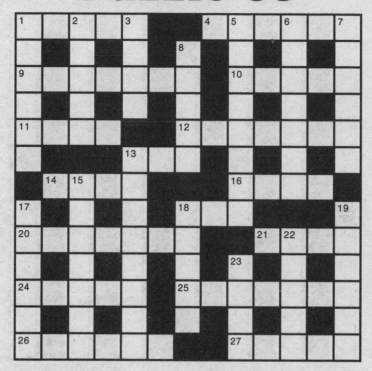

## Across

1. Bully (5)
4. Among (6)
9. Open framework (7)
10. Italian city (5)
11. Figure-skating jump (4)
12. Cyclone (7)
13. Demure (3)
14. Persian poet (4)
16. Motor car (4)
18. Pointed tool (3)
20. Extreme Liberal (7)
21. Needy (4)
24. Artless (5)
25. Brave (7)
26. Slip by (6)
27. Belgian battle (5)

## Down

1. Song (6)
2. Loosen (5)
3. Prepare for press (4)
5. Motherly (8)
6. Hibernating (7)
7. Sinew (6)
8. God (5)
13. Chirpy insects (8)
15. Sponge-cake (7)
17. Royal person (6)
18. Make parallel (5)
19. Caesar's murderer (6)
22. Elated (2,3)
23. Gambit or method used to achieve a particular result, especially in a game (4)

# Puzzle 34

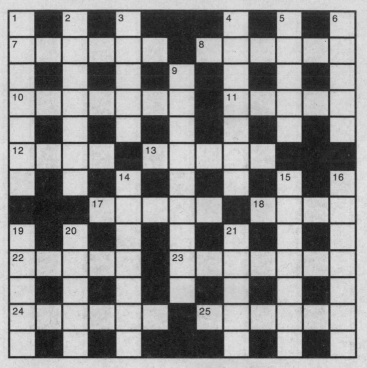

## Across

7. Property (6)
8. Steal cattle (6)
10. Pantries (7)
11. Greek area (5)
12. Horse breed (4)
13. Fireraising (5)
17. Strangle (5)
18. Celestial body (4)
22. Embrace (5)
23. Give life to (7)
24. Gentle teasing (6)
25. Feel contrition (6)

## Down

1. Rhyming slang word for a thief (3,4)
2. Immortal (7)
3. Anaesthetic (5)
4. Accounts checker (7)
5. Bear (5)
6. Foot lever (5)
9. Lambskin (9)
14. Part of book (7)
15. Wandered away (7)
16. Adriatic port (7)
19. Aqualung (5)
20. Pleasure trip (5)
21. Mean person (5)

  solution on page 181

# Puzzle 35

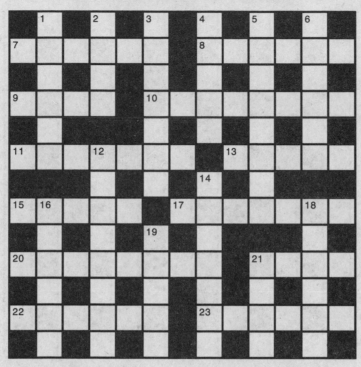

## Across

7. Visible suspension in the air (British, 6)
8. A shrine where a god is consulted (6)
9. Speak (4)
10. Jaunty (8)
11. Gliding on ice (7)
13. Exorbitant (5)
15. Shaving implement (5)
17. Thick heavy material with a raised pattern (7)
20. Reserved and uncommunicative (8)
21. Uncommon (4)
22. Constituent of concrete (6)
23. Raise in a relief (6)

## Down

1. Table linen material (6)
2. Written work (4)
3. A spear with three prongs (7)
4. Group who try actively to influence legislation (5)
5. Charismatic (8)
6. Large European food fish (6)
12. Double-crosser (3-5)
14. Bauble (7)
16. Rouse (6)
18. Compulsory force or threat (6)
19. Hearty (5)
21. Red gemstone (4)

# Puzzle 36

## Across

1. Thinly distributed (6)
4. Take a chance (6)
9. Gentlest (7)
10. Interior (5)
11. Protective covering of half-rotten vegetable matter (5)
12. Ankle-length black garment worn by a priest (7)
13. People who are almost identical to others (4,7)
18. Stuffy (atmosphere) (7)
20. Come up (5)
22. Mendacious (5)
23. Country dwelling (7)
24. Objective (6)
25. Method (6)

## Down

1. Seed often used on bread rolls (6)
2. Dire (5)
3. Was in an agitated emotional state (7)
5. Zodiacal constellation (5)
6. French word for "hello" (7)
7. Word uttered by Archimedes (6)
8. Creature with a long, twig-like body (5,6)
14. At a previous point in time (7)
15. Shockingly repellent (7)
16. Theatrical dance routine (6)
17. Save from sin (6)
19. Bird of prey (5)
21. Clumsy, ill-chosen (5)

**solution on page 181**

# Puzzle 37

## Across

1. Strong fence; for defense (8)
5. Piece of music (4)
9. An author's pseudonym (3,4)
11. Group of singers (5)
12. Friendly nation (4)
14. Baby's bed (3)
16. Side sheltered from wind (3)
18. Supply with notes (8)
20. Prejudice (4)
22. Sign of something about to happen (4)
23. A window in a roof (8)
24. Hawaiian floral garland (3)
25. Newt (3)
27. Farm outbuilding (4)
30. Shoot from a concealed position (5)
31. Moral (7)
33. Cast off (4)
34. Beneath the surface of the ocean (8)

## Down

1. Tubular wind instrument (4)
2. Characteristic language of a particular group (5)
3. Health resort (3)
4. Prearranged fight between two people (4)
6. Trouble (7)
7. Police or army officer (8)
8. Frosty (3)
10. Shrub often referred to as the tulip tree (8)
13. A party to a lawsuit (8)
15. Job (4)
17. Tall, tapering stone pillars (8)
19. Capacious bag or basket (4)
21. Fatuous (7)
26. Central point of concentration (5)
27. Honey-producing insect (3)
28. Part of horse's harness (4)
29. Humble request for help (4)
32. Garden tool (3)

solution on page 182

# Puzzle 38

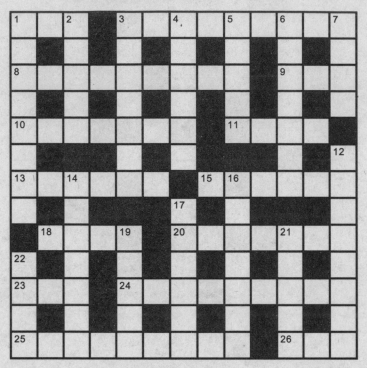

# Across

1. Diffident (3)
3. Marked by insufficient care or attention (9)
8. Check, investigate (9)
9. Large vase (3)
10. Thick spicy sauce (7)
11. Incursion (4)
13. Suitable for use as food (6)
15. Vocation (6)
18. Expired (4)
20. Dried out by heat (7)
23. Hard-shelled seed (3)
24. Black, heavily-flavored candy (9)
25. Capital of Romania (9)
26. Section of play (3)

# Down

1. Hand-held firework (8)
2. Wind-powered sailing vessel (5)
3. Small, arctic whale (7)
4. Clenches (6)
5. Nearer to the center (5)
6. Evasive (7)
7. Canvas shelter (4)
12. Slope (8)
14. Insanely irresponsible (7)
16. Airdrome (7)
17. Clouded (6)
19. The 4th letter of the Greek alphabet (5)
21. Port in north-western Israel on the Bay of Acre (5)
22. Rebuff (4)

solution on page 182

# Puzzle 39

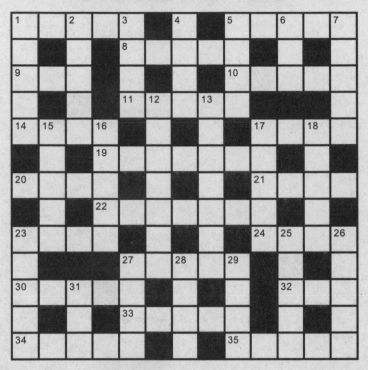

## Across

**1.** Popular fruit (5)
**5.** Military unit (5)
**8.** Relating to the countryside (5)
**9.** Paddle (3)
**10.** Make angry (5)
**11.** Hard slap (5)
**14.** Slippery fish (4)
**17.** Support for sails (4)
**19.** Branch of mathematics (7)
**20.** Statement of money owed (4)
**21.** Cogwheel (4)
**22.** Fit of temper (7)
**23.** Remain (4)
**24.** Cain's brother (4)
**27.** Realities (5)
**30.** Game with numbered balls (5)
**32.** Evil (3)
**33.** Strong and sharp (5)
**34.** Mutineer (5)
**35.** Panorama (5)

## Down

**1.** Higher up (5)
**2.** Hazard (5)
**3.** Makes a mistake (4)
**4.** Expanse (4)
**5.** Anti-aircraft fire (4)
**6.** Moved fast (3)
**7.** N African country (5)
**12.** Dark purple-red (7)
**13.** Series of acts at a night club (7)
**15.** Expel from one's property (5)
**16.** Saline (5)
**17.** Molten rock (5)
**18.** Ordered series (5)
**23.** Not affected by alcohol (5)
**25.** Holy book (5)
**26.** Soup serving spoon (5)
**27.** Young horse (4)
**28.** Birthday missive (4)
**29.** Soap froth (4)
**31.** Pen tip (3)

solution on page 182

# Puzzle 40

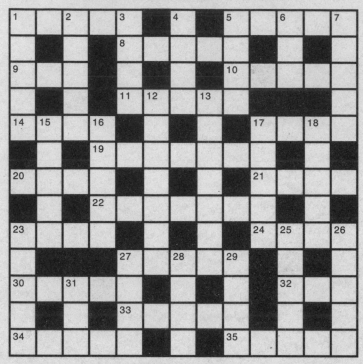

## Across

1. Great (5)
5. Former French coin (5)
8. Relating to a micro-organism (5)
9. Fitting (3)
10. Relating to sound (5)
11. Snappy (5)
14. Accepted (4)
17. Scottish lake (4)
19. Entangle (7)
20. Male red deer (4)
21. Lopsided (4)
22. White metallic element (7)
23. White substance beneath peel of fruit (4)
24. Domed recess (4)
27. Greek muse of lyric (5)
30. Once more (5)
32. Feeling of wonder (3)
33. Flow-control device (5)
34. Eskimo dog (5)
35. Period of darkness (5)

## Down

1. Smallest (5)
2. Proportion (5)
3. Regular (4)
4. Harvest (4)
5. Strip the skin off (4)
6. Sum up (3)
7. Material (5)
12. Parochial (7)
13. Keyboard player (7)
15. Giraffe-like creature (5)
16. Sailing vessel (5)
17. South American animal (5)
18. Army unit (5)
23. Cook in a simmering liquid (5)
25. Car crash (5)
26. Special occasion (5)
27. Feeling of grudging admiration and desire (4)
28. Competent (4)
29. Portent (4)
31. Beast of burden (3)

solution on page 183

# Puzzle 41

## Across

1. Heroic tale (4)
3. Most tranquil (7)
9. Slaughtered (9)
10. Lyric poem (3)
11. Red gemstone (4)
13. A disrespectful laugh (7)
15. The part of the stamen that bears pollen (6)
17. Dog-like (6)
19. Cut short (7)
20. Peak (4)
22. Horse of a dull brownish grey color (3)
23. Well-ordered (British, 9)
25. Listening (7)
26. Gyrate (4)

## Down

1. Identical (4)
2. Hydrogen, for instance (3)
4. Transversely (6)
5. Amber-colored dessert wine (7)
6. Store of items saved for future use (9)
7. Young child (4)
8. Apprentice (7)
12. Auditory communication (9)
14. A series of lines containing price information (3,4)
16. Beguile (7)
18. Vessel with a handle and spout; used to hold alcohol (usually wine) (6)
20. Skin problem (4)
21. Chief port of Yemen (4)
24. Plant fluid (3)

solution on page 183

# Puzzle 42

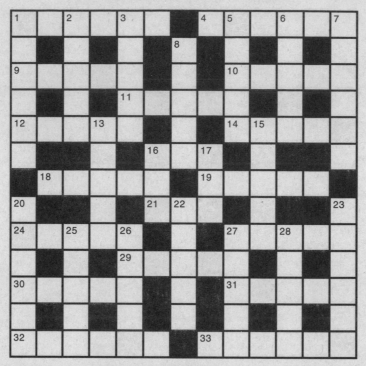

## Across

1. Weeping (6)
4. One who suffers for the sake of principle (6)
9. Happen (5)
10. Relating to the kidneys (5)
11. Pester (5)
12. Capture (5)
14. Written composition (5)
16. Color (3)
18. First letter of the Greek alphabet (5)
19. Mental representation (5)
21. Sharp explosive sound (3)
24. Vital liquid (5)
27. Allow in (5)
29. Join (5)
30. Earlier in time (5)
31. Smooth fabric (5)
32. Profoundly (6)
33. Verbal address (6)

## Down

1. Squat (6)
2. Racing vessel (5)
3. Compass point (5)
5. Correspond (5)
6. Hinged lifting tool (5)
7. Passes along (6)
8. Slacken off (5)
13. Dense growth of bushes or trees (5)
15. Place upright (5)
16. Gentle blow (3)
17. Duck (3)
20. Struck with a swinging motion (6)
22. Relating to sheep (5)
23. Stink (6)
25. Clan (5)
26. Relating to the countryside (5)
27. Greek storyteller (5)
28. Unit of length (British, 5)

# Puzzle 43

## Across

**1.** South American river (6)
**4.** Legendary king of the Britons (6)
**9.** Cut into small pieces (5)
**10.** Hand tool for measuring angles (5)
**11.** Residence (5)
**12.** Man-made fiber (5)
**14.** Engrave (5)
**16.** Took a meal (3)
**18.** Scrooge, for instance (5)
**19.** Stop sleeping (5)
**21.** The day before (3)
**24.** Hoard (5)
**27.** Joins in fabric (5)
**29.** Pointer (5)
**30.** Native New Zealander (5)
**31.** Deport from a country (5)
**32.** N American native dog (6)
**33.** Choice (6)

## Down

**1.** Oval-shaped nut (6)
**2.** Declare invalid (5)
**3.** Large body of water (5)
**5.** Medieval musical instrument (5)
**6.** Be suspended in the air (5)
**7.** Substitute (6)
**8.** Projecting nose (5)
**13.** Fertile tract in desert (5)
**15.** Joint of the leg (5)
**16.** Unit of surface area equal to 100 square meters (3)
**17.** Female sheep (3)
**20.** Road surfacing material (6)
**22.** Poetry (5)
**23.** Towards the tail of a ship (6)
**25.** Acute pain (5)
**26.** Canonized person (5)
**27.** Clean with a broom (5)
**28.** Excuse (5)

solution on page 184

# Puzzle 44

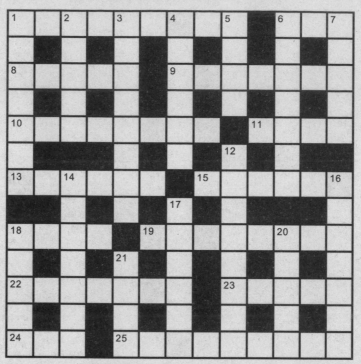

## Across

**1.** Alliance (9)
**6.** Male cat (3)
**8.** Phoney (5)
**9.** Swordplay (7)
**10.** Showing good spirits (8)
**11.** Smut from a fire (4)
**13.** Requiring less effort (6)
**15.** Run very fast, usually for a short distance (6)
**18.** Financial institution (4)
**19.** Fortified place where troops are stationed (8)
**22.** US Grand Canyon State (7)
**23.** In the middle of (5)
**24.** Side sheltered from wind (3)
**25.** Most lustrous (9)

## Down

**1.** Booth (7)
**2.** Slant (5)
**3.** Enclosed (8)
**4.** The process of flowing in (6)
**5.** Not any (4)
**6.** Capital of Libya (7)
**7.** Could (5)
**12.** Come near (8)
**14.** Daybreak (7)
**16.** This evening (7)
**17.** Hunting expedition (6)
**18.** Noisy fight (5)
**20.** Tea-time sweet bread roll (5)
**21.** Explosive device (4)

solution on page 184

# Puzzle 45

## Across

1. Stabbing weapon (6)
4. Barbaric (6)
7. Large and showy garden plant (9)
9. Chopper (3)
10. Vase (3)
11. Writing fluid (3)
14. The first garden (4)
15. Beguiling (8)
17. Pace (5)
18. Perfidy (8)
19. Young sheep (4)
21. Darken (3)
22. Zodiacal lion (3)
24. Listening organ (3)
25. Nanny (9)
28. City in SW Switzerland (6)
29. Son of one's brother or sister (6)

## Down

1. Impairment (6)
2. Wildebeest (3)
3. Oil purification plant (8)
4. Sluggish (4)
5. Contend (3)
6. Creamy, alcoholic drink (6)
7. Choice (9)
8. Chewed over (9)
12. Work dough (5)
13. Young goat (3)
16. Amulet (8)
17. Revenue (3)
18. Be owned by (6)
20. Tunnel (6)
23. Continent (4)
26. Consumption (3)
27. Pixie (3)

solution on page 184

# Puzzle 46

## Across

1. Melted (6)
4. Losing water (6)
7. Bangles (9)
9. Listening organ (3)
10. Vase (3)
11. Employ (3)
14. Expired (4)
15. Occurrence (8)
17. Supreme Teutonic god (5)
18. Sheets and pillowcases (3-5)
19. Capital of Norway (4)
21. Fishing implement (3)
22. Uncooked (3)
24. Very small circular shape (3)
25. Discuss terms of an arrangement (9)
28. Not so cold (6)
29. It's XI in Roman numerals (6)

## Down

1. Yarn (6)
2. Armed struggle (3)
3. Conclusion (8)
4. Child's toy (4)
5. All the same (3)
6. Semi-precious gemstone (6)
7. Cessation of normal operation (9)
8. Take the place of (9)
12. Enroll (5)
13. Alcoholic spirit (3)
16. Declare to be a saint (8)
17. Synthetic hairpiece (3)
18. Market trader's cart (6)
20. Receive (6)
23. Having little money (4)
26. Tree (3)
27. Golf-peg (3)

 solution on page 185

# Puzzle 47

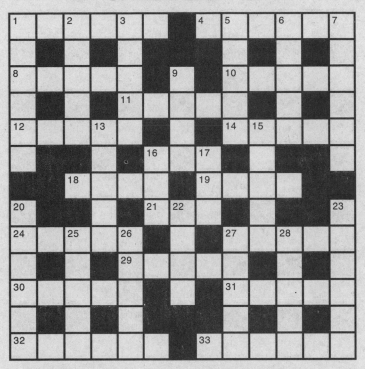

## Across

1. Type of brandy (6)
4. Correspond to (6)
8. Estimate (5)
10. Young eel (5)
11. Accumulate (5)
12. Ameliorate (5)
14. Sharp, hooked claw (5)
16. Single (3)
18. Always (4)
19. Calf meat (4)
21. Female sheep (3)
24. Might (5)
27. Deep brown (5)
29. Happen again (5)
30. Eskimo hut (5)
31. Ruffian (5)
32. Leash (6)
33. Reply (6)

## Down

1. Young swan (6)
2. Groove (5)
3. In the lead (5)
5. Mission (5)
6. Blacksmith's tool (5)
7. Trip (6)
9. Admonish (4)
13. Fresh (5)
15. Concern (5)
16. Mineral (3)
17. First woman (3)
20. Actor's notes (6)
22. Taper (4)
23. Supplication (6)
25. Dark (5)
26. Male bee (5)
27. Of the city (5)
28. Beneath (5)

# Puzzle 48

## Across

**1.** Remind (6)
**5.** Large shrimp sauteed in butter and garlic (6)
**8.** Exposed (4)
**9.** Pinioned (8)
**10.** Cunningly (5)
**11.** Attentive (7)
**14.** Someone who makes an offer (6)
**15.** Tastelessly showy (6)
**17.** Banqueted (7)
**19.** Bother (5)
**21.** Triumphant (8)
**23.** Metal joint formed by softening with heat and fusing together (4)
**24.** Sorrowful through loss or deprivation (6)
**25.** Illness (6)

## Down

**2.** Repugnant (9)
**3.** Jumbled, mixed (7)
**4.** Undertaking (4)
**5.** Collect discarded material (8)
**6.** Sought an answer to (5)
**7.** Pastry dish (3)
**12.** Not sullied (9)
**13.** A man-made object (8)
**16.** Replenishment (7)
**18.** Grab (5)
**20.** The tube of a tobacco pipe (4)
**22.** Expend (3)

**solution on page 185**

# Puzzle 49

This one will take a bit of thinking about... The solutions to the Across clues should be entered into the grid in the traditional way, but those to the Down clues should be entered upside down. We've filled in the first, as an example.

# Across

1. Put into code (7)
5. Units of electrical power (5)
8. Maiden name indicator (3)
9. Certification (7)
10. Strain (5)
11. Very small circular shape (3)
13. Voided (9)
15. Endeavor (6)
17. Favor (6)
20. Musical accompaniment to a vocal piece (9)
21. Reposed (3)

23. Shop selling milk, butter, etc (5)
25. Time between one event and another (7)
26. Have (3)
27. UK racecourse (5)
28. Clap (7)

# Down

1. Evade (5)
2. Subject (5)
3. Detailed list of items in stock (9)
4. Flexible (6)
5. Join together with thread (3)

6. Most impartial (7)
7. Make amends for (7)
12. As well (3)
14. Jar of mixed flower petals and spices (3-6)
15. Taxing to the utmost (7)
16. Mountaineer (7)
18. Alcoholic beverage (3)
19. Beast (6)
21. Month (5)
22. Figure representing the human form (5)
24. Plaything (3)

# Puzzle 50

## Across

1. Black-and-white striped equine (5)
3. 'Fab' group associated with the 1960s (7)
6. Cut back (7)
8. Immature insect (5)
10. Showiness (11)
12. Long-eared creature, similar to rabbit (4)
13. Digression (5)
15. Monk's cubicle (4)
17. Scene of conflict (11)
19. Military trainee (5)
20. Common farmyard bird (7)
21. Instrument for measuring the angle between stars (7)
22. Combine (5)

## Down

1. City in Switzerland (6)
2. Russian unit of currency (6)
3. Unsound (3)
4. Jeweled head-dress (5)
5. Very frightened (6)
7. Ensnarled (8)
9. Popular pond creature (8)
10. Forepart (5)
11. Nude (5)
14. Calculating machine (6)
15. Hackneyed saying (6)
16. Airport waiting area (6)
18. Delicacy (5)
20. Feline mammal (3)

solution on page 186

# Puzzle 51

## Across

1. Jester (5)
3. Division of a book (7)
6. Beaming (7)
8. Trick (5)
10. Elaborated (11)
12. Close (4)
13. Narrow backstreet (5)
15. Gentle blows (4)
17. E.g. New Year's Day, etc (4-7)
19. Avid (5)
20. Pin used in bowling (7)
21. Sauce served with fish (British, 7)
22. Intense (5)

## Down

1. Lingo (6)
2. Newspaper chief (6)
3. Feline mammal (3)
4. Black and white, bamboo-eating mammal (5)
5. Draw back (6)
7. Mr Bonaparte (8)
9. Verse of five lines (8)
10. Bedroom on a ship (5)
11. This current period in time (5)
14. Missing (6)
15. Maneuver (6)
16. Strategy (6)
18. Went down on the knees (5)
20. Her (3)

# Puzzle 52

## Across

1. Cost (5)
4. Sincere (7)
7. Time of celebration (6)
10. Graven image (4)
12. Animal (5)
13. Hire (5)
14. Lip (3)
15. Corrode, as with acid (4)
16. Bullfighter (7)
19. Lucky charm (6)
20. Vocalizations (6)
23. Elongate (7)
25. Without hair (4)
27. Chap (3)
28. Musical composition (5)
29. Biting flies (5)
31. Blast (4)
32. Strip (6)
33. Slowly (7)
34. Imitate (5)

## Down

1. Difficulty (7)
2. Thought (4)
3. Orient (4)
4. Protective fold of skin (6)
5. Sound (5)
6. Cultivated soil (5)
8. Gelatin (5)
9. Got rid of (7)
11. Come away (6)
14. Perturbed (7)
16. Sacred songs (6)
17. Type of lettuce (3)
18. Decompose (3)
21. Images (5)
22. Caused by earth vibration (7)
24. Sign (6)
25. Intolerant person (5)
26. Loved (5)
29. Minute life-form (4)
30. Particle (4)

solution on page 187

# Puzzle 53

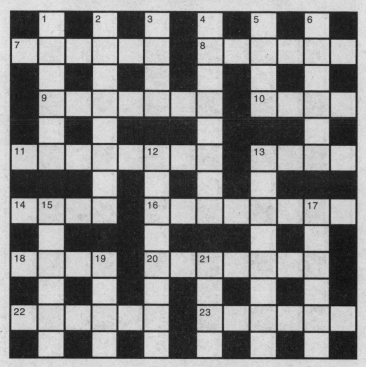

## Across

**7.** Dozen (6)
**8.** Bowman (6)
**9.** Send another way (7)
**10.** North American lake (4)
**11.** British poet (8)
**13.** Child's toy (4)
**14.** Master of ceremonies (4)
**16.** Hypersensitive (8)
**18.** Post (4)
**20.** Phlegm (7)
**22.** Shelled, aquatic reptile (6)
**23.** Ribbon-like strip of pasta (6)

## Down

**1.** Veer (6)
**2.** Reed instrument (8)
**3.** Bill of fare (4)
**4.** Characteristic of a mother (8)
**5.** Disease of the skin (4)
**6.** Antenna (6)
**12.** Looked for (8)
**13.** A place in which photographs are developed (8)
**15.** Not clear (6)
**17.** Breathe in (6)
**19.** Tardy (4)
**21.** Collapsible shelter (4)

solution on page 187

# Puzzle 54

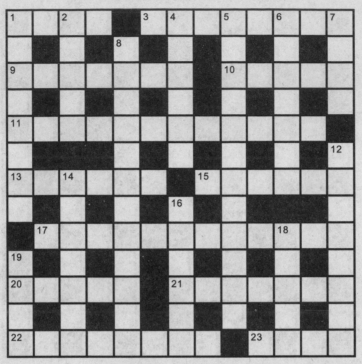

## Across

1. Wound made by cutting (4)
3. Not appropriate for a purpose or occasion (8)
9. Blink (7)
10. Unit of length (British, 5)
11. A crime less serious than a felony (British, 12)
13. Involuntary vibration (6)
15. Person who tends fires (6)
17. Sanctification (12)
20. Animated (5)
21. Woman's sleeveless undergarment (7)
22. Threatening or foreshadowing evil (8)
23. Pixies (4)

## Down

1. Maker or repairer of firearms (8)
2. Items of footwear (5)
4. More modest (6)
5. Argued in protest or opposition (12)
6. Whatever happens to be available especially when offered to an unexpected guest (3,4)
7. Stench (4)
8. Excessive desire to eat (12)
12. Daughter of a sovereign (8)
14. Eating away (7)
16. Frozen spike of water (6)
18. Dialect (5)
19. Bulk (4)

solution on page 187

# Puzzle 55

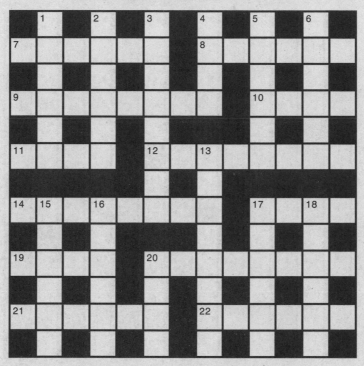

## Across

**7.** Dog house (6)
**8.** Rhododendron-like shrub (6)
**9.** Intellectuals (8)
**10.** Corrosive compound (4)
**11.** Listen (4)
**12.** Distinguish (8)
**14.** Having no weak points (8)
**17.** As well (4)
**19.** Explosive device (4)
**20.** Chance event (8)
**21.** Photographic equipment (6)
**22.** Silvery metallic element (6)

## Down

**1.** Hound dog (6)
**2.** Mainstay (6)
**3.** Washing (8)
**4.** Sea fish (4)
**5.** Without an occupant (6)
**6.** Notion, tenet (6)
**13.** Tempting (8)
**15.** Line on weather map (6)
**16.** Pill (6)
**17.** Kidnap (6)
**18.** Vocalist (6)
**20.** Not at home (4)

# Puzzle 56

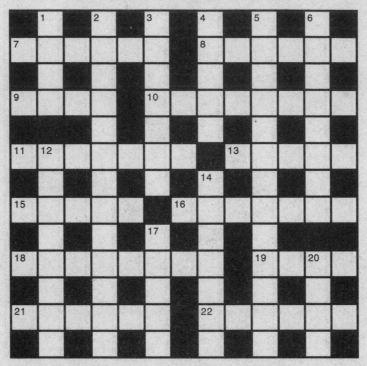

## Across

7. Dock (6)
8. Stopped (6)
9. Long narrative poem (4)
10. Rescue vessel (8)
11. Intransigent (7)
13. Start (5)
15. Measured steps (5)
16. Luggage (7)
18. Fairly (8)
19. Waistband (4)
21. Hunting bird (6)
22. Contrite (6)

## Down

1. Distort (4)
2. Perimeter (13)
3. Band of flowers (7)
4. Budge (5)
5. Dumbfounded (13)
6. Loosening up (8)
12. Slanted (8)
14. Collection of electrical cells (7)
17. Consider (5)
20. Eschew (4)

solution on page 188

# Puzzle 57

## Across

**1.** Timid (3)
**3.** Rushing down in torrents (9)
**8.** Find out (9)
**9.** Diagrammatic representation of an area (3)
**10.** Salad vegetable (7)
**11.** Measure of three feet (4)
**13.** Sound powers of mind (6)
**15.** Inn (6)
**18.** Grew older (4)
**20.** Burst inward (7)
**23.** Employ (3)
**24.** Fake (9)
**25.** Object that orbits around the earth (9)
**26.** Fetch (3)

## Down

**1.** Most minor (8)
**2.** Racing vessel (5)
**3.** Path for electrical current (7)
**4.** Very frightened (6)
**5.** Irritate (5)
**6.** Plunge (7)
**7.** Expression of open-mouthed astonishment (4)
**12.** Cyberspace (8)
**14.** Disuse (7)
**16.** Mollify (7)
**17.** Two-piece bathing suit (6)
**19.** Bore a hole (5)
**21.** Due (5)
**22.** Bother (4)

**solution on page 188**

# Puzzle 58

## Across

**1.** Manufacturing plant (7)
**4.** Evil spirit (5)
**7.** Less dangerous (5)
**10.** Sticker (5)
**11.** Nocturnal bird of prey (3)
**12.** Scottish port (3)
**13.** Decompose (5)
**14.** Keen (5)
**16.** Glass vessel (6)
**18.** On the move (6)
**22.** Step (5)
**24.** Inexpensive (5)
**26.** Menagerie (3)
**27.** Painting, sculpture, etc (3)
**28.** Foyer (5)
**29.** Eskimo's home (5)

**31.** Papa (5)
**32.** Giant planet (7)

## Down

**1.** Welded together (5)
**2.** Foot digit (3)
**3.** Shouted (6)
**4.** Correct errors in computer program code (5)
**5.** Grinding tooth (5)
**6.** Tell a story (7)
**8.** Aspect (5)
**9.** Imperial (5)
**15.** Consume (3)
**16.** Short-winged hawk (7)
**17.** Young child (3)
**19.** Prickly plants (5)
**20.** Perfect (5)

**21.** Wax drawing implement (6)
**22.** Firm (5)
**23.** Monastery (5)
**25.** Dig into (5)
**30.** Intestines (3)

**solution on page 189**

# Puzzle 59

The answers in this crossword are anagrams of their clues, but can you discover the correct anagram in every case? (For instance, the solution to a clue such as 'Adder' could be either 'Dared' or 'Dread'... the choice isn't always obvious!)

## Across

- **1.** In jot (5)
- **4.** Drag bin (7)
- **8.** A loss (5)
- **9.** Eat rope (7)
- **10.** Sell sin (7)
- **11.** End me (5)
- **12.** A worry (6)
- **14.** Guiana (6)
- **18.** He fit (5)
- **20.** Ape myth (7)
- **22.** Aces top (7)
- **23.** To hop (5)
- **24.** Dire use (7)
- **25.** I sell (5)

## Down

- **1.** Jot lily (7)
- **2.** Sun lair (7)
- **3.** Voter (5)
- **4.** Sip boy (6)
- **5.** Beg rice (7)
- **6.** At age (5)
- **7.** Adder (5)
- **13.** Handoff (7)
- **15.** It's a con (7)
- **16.** One army (7)
- **17.** See Les (6)
- **18.** Trout (5)
- **19.** It's me (5)
- **21.** Appal (5)

solution on page 189

# Puzzle 60

## Across

**1.** Not dense (6)
**4.** Slip away (6)
**8.** Asian country (5)
**10.** Ascent (5)
**11.** Tea-time sweet bread roll (5)
**12.** Band around a horse's belly (5)
**14.** Inclined to anger or bad feelings (5)
**16.** Brownie (3)
**18.** Languish (4)
**19.** Reverberate (4)
**21.** Depressed (3)
**24.** Very light brown (5)
**27.** Pasture (5)
**29.** Monarch (5)
**30.** Unit of weight (5)
**31.** Nimble (5)
**32.** Spin around (6)
**33.** Mastermind (6)

## Down

**1.** Not generous (6)
**2.** British snake (5)
**3.** Strong sweeping cut (5)
**5.** Tying cords (5)
**6.** Head of a religious order (5)
**7.** Fertilized egg (6)
**9.** Painful sore (4)
**13.** Object (5)
**15.** Guide (5)
**16.** Slippery fish (3)
**17.** Not many (3)
**20.** Four-sided shape (6)
**22.** Greasy (4)
**23.** Evaluate (6)
**25.** Nearer to the center (5)
**26.** Vertical (5)
**27.** Vine fruit (5)
**28.** Excuse (5)

**solution on page 189**

# Puzzle 61

## Across

1. Dialect (6)
4. System (6)
8. Crisp bread (5)
10. Lure (5)
11. Senior (5)
12. Greenfly, for instance (5)
14. Common viper (5)
16. Yes (3)
18. Peak (4)
19. Peruse (4)
21. The 7th letter of the Greek alphabet (3)
24. Fully grown (5)
27. Demise (5)
29. Daisy-like flower (5)
30. Departs (5)
31. Foreign (5)
32. Jerked (6)
33. Dog-like (6)

## Down

1. Real (6)
2. Single story bus (5)
3. Observed (5)
5. Additional (5)
6. Warm and damp (atmosphere) (5)
7. Dissuades (6)
9. Jumpy (4)
13. Force (5)
15. Male duck (5)
16. Bladed, chopping tool (3)
17. Time period (3)
20. Bread shop (6)
22. London art gallery (4)
23. Accidental (6)
25. Coupling (5)
26. Appreciation (5)
27. Play (5)
28. Excuse (5)

solution on page 190

# Puzzle 62

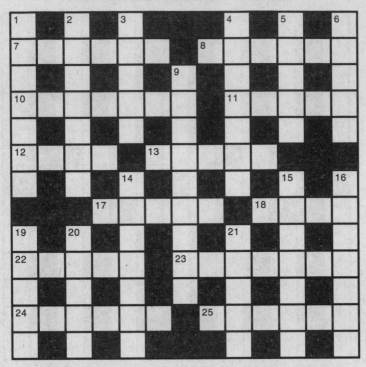

## Across

7. Group of six (6)
8. Skinny British 1960s model (6)
10. Wild and disorderly (7)
11. The place at which (5)
12. Yuletide (4)
13. Hair on the chin (5)
17. Sphere (5)
18. Crooked (4)
22. Muslim religion (5)
23. Made of clay (7)
24. Smear with ointment (6)
25. Beetle (6)

## Down

1. Minimal underwear item (1-6)
2. Laid bare (7)
3. Citrus fruit (5)
4. Clumsy (7)
5. Monsters (5)
6. French school (5)
9. Met (9)
14. Sustenance (7)
15. Breed of fowl (7)
16. Substitute on hand (5-2)
19. Parson (5)
20. Distribute (5)
21. Instant (5)

solution on page 190

# Puzzle 63

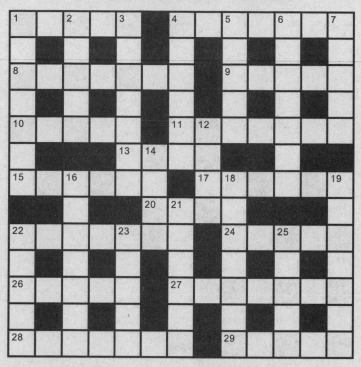

## Across

1. Duffer (5)
4. In the news (7)
8. Unrifled firearm (7)
9. Celtic priest (5)
10. Per ardua ad —— (5)
11. Put in the shadow (7)
13. Roman emperor (4)
15. Martial art (6)
17. Forced out (6)
20. Mouth parts (4)
22. Opposed to (7)
24. Extreme (5)
26. Repair (5)
27. Plover (7)
28. Locally prevalent (7)
29. Reigned (5)

## Down

1. Russian (7)
2. German sub (1-4)
3. Elaborate spectacle (7)
4. Frail (6)
5. Foot lever (5)
6. Griddle cake (7)
7. Gatehouse (5)
12. Cage (4)
14. Slippery fish (4)
16. Responded (7)
18. Supplanter (7)
19. Pulled (7)
21. Sloping print (6)
22. Capacious (5)
23. Prophet (5)
25. Musical warble (5)

solution on page 190

# Puzzle 64

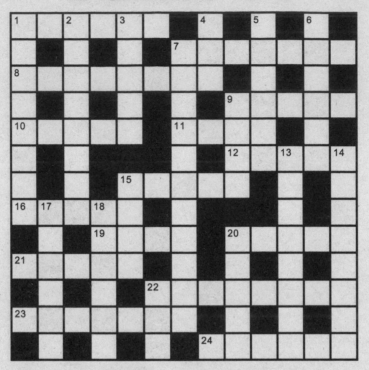

## Across

1. Shrew (6)
7. Gruesome (7)
8. Criminal (8)
9. Position taken (5)
10. Utterly defeats (5)
11. Chilly (4)
12. Confused scuffle (5)
15. For this reason (5)
16. Tuscan city (5)
19. Affirm (4)
20. Side of cut gem (5)
21. Clay pigment (5)
22. Merrymaker (8)
23. Puts on (7)
24. Sacredly obscure (6)

## Down

1. Energetic (8)
2. Forgo (8)
3. Blows (5)
4. Road vehicle (3)
5. Chatter (6)
6. EC member (6)
7. Hired fighters (11)
9. A number (4)
13. Guinevere's lover (8)
14. Secret (8)
15. Possess (4)
17. Earnings (6)
18. Thin (6)
20. Flaming (5)
22. King (3)

# Puzzle 65

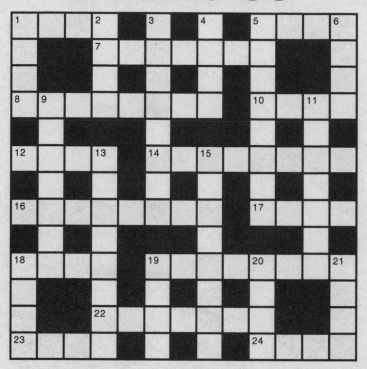

## Across

1. Market (4)
5. Compass point (4)
7. Spherical organ of vision (7)
8. Impasse (8)
10. Bloodstained (4)
12. Second-hand (4)
14. Simplicity (8)
16. Mining waste hill (4,4)
17. Needle-case (4)
18. Early bet (4)
19. Mayfly (8)
22. Image boost (3-4)
23. Handle roughly (4)
24. Nervous (4)

## Down

1. Female servant (4)
2. Incline (4)
3. Paraffin oil (8)
4. Bundle (4)
5. Refinement (8)
6. Minute (4)
9. Greek letter (7)
11. Savior (7)
13. Poor verse (8)
15. Precious stone (8)
18. First human (4)
19. Island (4)
20. Fret (4)
21. Land force (4)

solution on page 191

# Puzzle 66

## Across

4. Deceive (6)
5. Therefore (4)
7. Coaxed (7)
10. Express (5)
11. Break up (7)
12. Regretful (5)
14. Morsels (7)
15. Welcome (5)
16. Express strong disapproval of (7)
20. Dodge (5)
21. Lands (7)
22. At high volume (4)
23. Immature (6)

## Down

1. Deluge (5)
2. Borders (5)
3. Slum areas (7)
4. Expensive (4)
6. Fortified wine (6)
8. Restricted (7)
9. Slaver (7)
10. Arrogant (7)
13. Abase oneself (6)
14. Tiresome (7)
17. —— Wilde; playwright (5)
18. Legionary emblem (5)
19. Cat's cry (4)

**solution on page 191**

# Puzzle 67

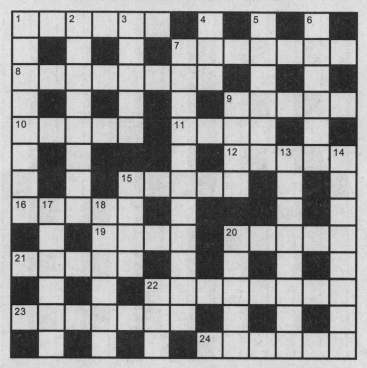

## Across

1. Place of learning (6)
7. Original disciple (7)
8. Idiom (8)
9. Move to music (5)
10. Armistice (5)
11. Jump (4)
12. Eerie (5)
15. Spice (5)
16. Mountain call (5)
19. Animal's den (4)
20. Scent (5)
21. Material for jeans (5)
22. Ocean (8)
23. Oval (7)
24. Beautiful women (6)

## Down

1. Beneficial (8)
2. Esteemed (British, 8)
3. Undeveloped seed (5)
4. Mimic (3)
5. Break free (6)
6. Machine for chopping bacon (6)
7. A volcanic rock (11)
9. Daybreak (4)
13. Forever (8)
14. Simple cranes (8)
15. Shellfish (4)
17. Excessively (6)
18. Evoke (6)
20. Laminated rock (5)
22. Snake (3)

**solution on page 192**

# Puzzle 68

## Across

1. Predatory animal (6)
4. French naval base (5)
8. Divide (5)
9. Dirigible (7)
10. Became invalid (7)
11. Clay (anagram) (4)
12. Hitherto (3)
14. London district (4)
15. Mountain range (4)
18. Scarlet (3)
21. Slippery fish (4)
23. Draw out (7)
25. Tropical fruit (7)
26. Foremost (5)
27. Verse (5)
28. Arm covering (6)

## Down

1. Court clown (6)
2. West Indian song (7)
3. Previous (8)
4. Prickly seed-case (4)
5. Moral (5)
6. Alcoholic liquor (6)
7. Fop (5)
13. Pleasing (8)
16. Grassy plain (7)
17. Mend (6)
19. English novelist (5)
20. Sculpture (6)
22. Dotty, mad, loopy (5)
24. Lady (4)

solution on page 192

# Puzzle 69

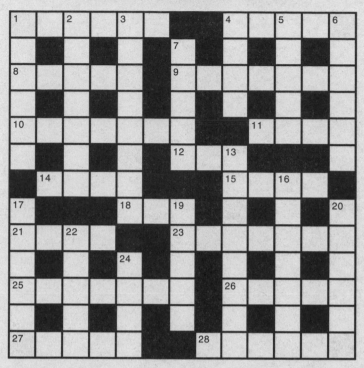

## Across

1. Money-holder (6)
4. Breadth (5)
8. Love affair (5)
9. Type of trout (7)
10. Partly coincide (7)
11. Fruit (4)
12. Pitch (3)
14. Offshore area (4)
15. Biblical garden (4)
18. Pluto (3)
21. Cotton (4)
23. Acorn plant (3-4)
25. Cosa Nostra members (7)
26. Level betting (5)
27. Fashion (5)
28. Crystalline compound (6)

## Down

1. Means of attack (6)
2. Big cat (7)
3. Registered (8)
4. Linger (4)
5. Correct program faults (5)
6. US state (6)
7. Church cellar (5)
13. Rash (8)
16. Fervent (7)
17. Feathers (6)
19. Of sound (5)
20. Diminish (6)
22. Agile (5)
24. Fret (4)

solution on page 192

# Puzzle 70

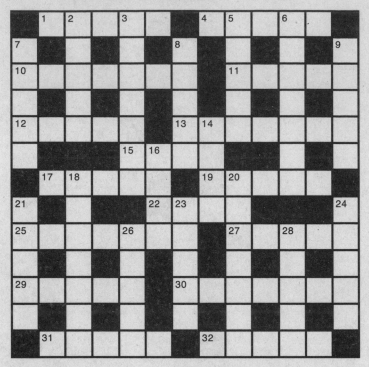

## Across

1. Military fabric (5)
4. Cut of beef (1-4)
10. Transmitted (7)
11. Loud (5)
12. Set of beliefs (5)
13. Nematode (7)
15. Bitter sweet (4)
17. Comply (5)
19. Watering-hole (5)
22. Possesses (4)
25. Flight-operating company (7)
27. Hurry (5)
29. Belgian city (5)
30. Muffling (7)
31. Declare (5)
32. Grown-up (5)

## Down

2. Cut in two (5)
3. Tonic (7)
5. Hackneyed (5)
6. Kenyan capital (7)
7. Wagon (5)
8. Layabout (5)
9. Diminutive native (5)
14. Famous English school (4)
16. Vast age (4)
18. Item of clothing (7)
20. Embarrassed (7)
21. Arctic marten (5)
23. Of poor stature (5)
24. Integrate (5)
26. Dormant (5)
28. Eddy (5)

solution on page 193

# Puzzle 71

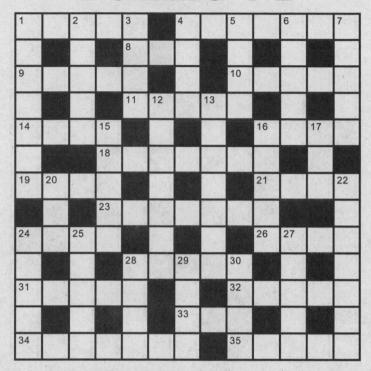

One of the words listed against each clue number is the solution to be entered into the crossword—but which one? The choice is yours…

## Across

1. Focus; Laces (5)
4. Spangle; Swindle (7)
8. Top; Cup (3)
9. Llama; Tiara (5)
10. Scant; Steam (5)
11. Broth; Ratio (5)
14. Hope; Hump (4)
16. Idle; User (4)
18. Arrived; Artisan (7)
19. Dens; Dabs (4)
21. Deaf; Leaf (4)
23. Edifice; Edition (7)
24. Hell; Well (4)
26. Tags; Rags (4)
28. Beset; Beret (5)
31. There; Tiara (5)
32. Alibi; Align (5)
33. Nun; Sun (3)
34. Matches; Hatched (7)
35. Glean; First (5)

## Down

1. Latches; Filched (7)
2. Chasm; Clamp (5)
3. Scar; Stir (4)
4. Slot; Spot (4)
5. Idle; Also (4)
6. Grass; Crate (5)
7. Enter; Ended (5)
12. Airline; Airport (7)
13. Invoice; Involve (7)
15. Easel; Nasal (5)
16. Udder; Utter (5)
17. Era; Ear (3)
20. Age; Ego (3)
22. Fashion; Leaders (7)
24. Watch; Mulch (5)
25. Meant; Leant (5)
27. Oxide; Agile (5)
28. Hash; Bath (4)
29. Send; Sent (4)
30. Rang; Tang (4)

# Puzzle 72

## Across

1. Adolescent (8)
5. Very cold (4)
8. Standard items worn by schoolchildren, for example (8)
9. Charitable gifts (4)
11. Entertainment highlight (4-7)
14. Long period of time (3)
16. Heather (5)
17. Source of metal (3)
18. Rebuked (11)
21. Man-eating giant (4)
22. Merrymaker (8)
24. Slippery fish (4)
25. Unfaithfulness in marriage (8)

## Down

1. Tightly-drawn (4)
2. Sends forth (5)
3. Contrite (10)
4. Forest tree (3)
6. W Indian song (7)
7. Confusion (8)
10. Actor-singer, and star of 'Dallas' (6,4)
12. Hindu deity (5)
13. Dreadful (8)
15. Clothing (7)
19. Research (5)
20. Ancient city (4)
23. Finish (3)

**solution on page 193**

# Puzzle 73

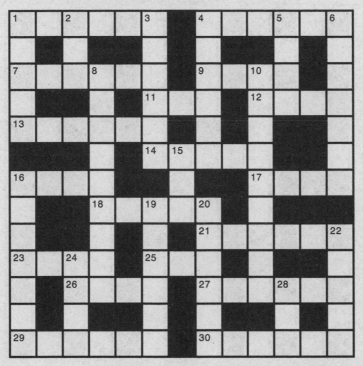

## Across

**1.** Shocked (6)
**4.** Judgmental reviewer (6)
**7.** Make certain of (6)
**9.** Transported (4)
**11.** Club (3)
**12.** Monetary unit used by some countries of the EC (4)
**13.** Woman often in distress? (6)
**14.** Lofty nest of a bird of prey (5)
**16.** Female operatic star (4)
**17.** Magnitude (4)
**18.** Cook in an oven (5)
**21.** Vehicle for carrying a coffin (6)
**23.** Tiny hole in skin (4)
**25.** Consumption (3)
**26.** Chances (4)
**27.** Implement for cutting grass (6)
**29.** Corpulent (6)
**30.** Sordid (6)

## Down

**1.** Honor (5)
**2.** Owns (3)
**3.** Threefold (6)
**4.** Wheel on a leg of furniture (6)
**5.** Ballet skirt (4)
**6.** Unit of heat, often applied to a foodstuff (7)
**8.** Without a blemish (9)
**10.** Essential (9)
**15.** Affirmative word (3)
**16.** Abandon hope (7)
**19.** Entertained (6)
**20.** Dissertation (6)
**22.** Each one, without exception (5)
**24.** Defeat in battle (4)
**28.** Popular beverage (3)

**solution on page 194**

# Puzzle 74

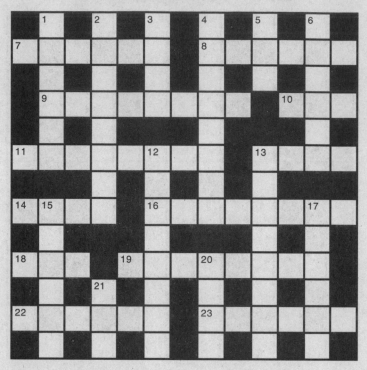

## Across

**7.** Almost (6)
**8.** Area surrounded by water (6)
**9.** Mercy (8)
**10.** Command (3)
**11.** Badge (8)
**13.** Lose heat (4)
**14.** Apiece (4)
**16.** Part of bed (8)
**18.** Travelers' pub (3)
**19.** Opposite words (8)
**22.** Young swan (6)
**23.** Adhered (6)

## Down

**1.** Sri Lanka's former name (6)
**2.** Flourish (8)
**3.** Cattle shed (4)
**4.** Form of transport (8)
**5.** Go by 4 Down (3)
**6.** Dark blue color (6)
**12.** Propose (8)
**13.** Transporting (8)
**15.** Vexes (6)
**17.** County (6)
**20.** Globes (4)
**21.** Come to a halt (3)

solution on page 194

# Puzzle 75

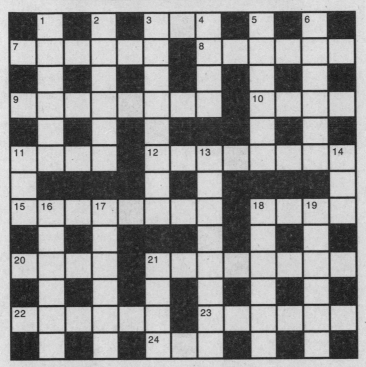

## Across

3. In the past (3)
7. Dictates (6)
8. Woody tropical grass (6)
9. Drink (8)
10. First man (4)
11. Make tight (4)
12. Effervesced (8)
15. Captive (8)
18. Mentally healthy (4)
20. Walk through water (4)
21. Major center of the French wine trade (8)
22. Vocation (6)
23. Broke down (6)
24. Outfit (3)

## Down

1. Change to ice (6)
2. Rescind (6)
3. Hired murderer (8)
4. Woodwind instrument (4)
5. Go on board (6)
6. Revolve (6)
11. Plant juice (3)
13. Plane (8)
14. Colorant (3)
16. 40th US President (6)
17. Spit for holding meat in place (6)
18. Having a beautiful, natural view (6)
19. Sickness (6)
21. Sound made by a dog (4)

solution on page 194

# Puzzle 76

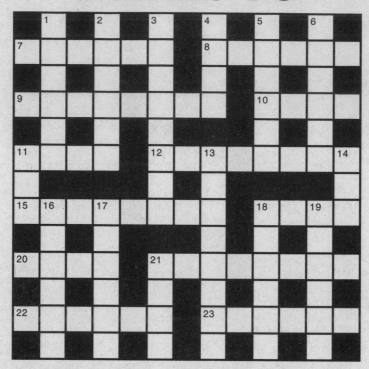

## Across

7. Objective (6)
8. Retaliate (6)
9. Woodland flower (8)
10. Stated (4)
11. Rivet (4)
12. Grisly (8)
15. Note in music equal to half a minim (8)
18. Like (4)
20. Prod (4)
21. Mexican hat (8)
22. Traditional Christmas songs (6)
23. Walk silently (6)

## Down

1. Vote (6)
2. Consented (6)
3. Durability (8)
4. Lavish formal dance (4)
5. Population count (6)
6. Self-centeredness (6)
11. Pocket (3)
13. Utmost (8)
14. Stretch (3)
16. Do again (6)
17. Overwhelming fear (6)
18. Abrade (6)
19. Vegetable, also known as squash (6)
21. Waistband (4)

solution on page 195

PUZZLES

# Puzzle 77

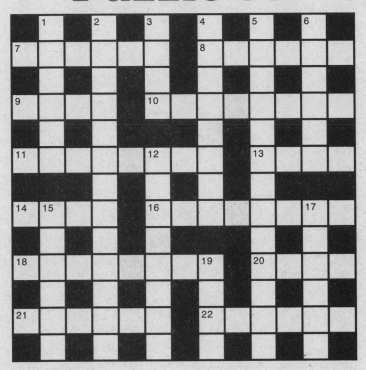

## Across

**7.** Sweet-talked (6)
**8.** Beginner (6)
**9.** Wise Men (4)
**10.** Minor celestial body composed of rock and metal (8)
**11.** Professional care for the fingernails (8)
**13.** Pal, chum (4)
**14.** Minicab (4)
**16.** Mediterranean island, west of Italy (8)
**18.** Natural spring (8)
**20.** Hostelries (4)
**21.** Bother (6)
**22.** Wriggle (6)

## Down

**1.** Musical composition (6)
**2.** Attention-seeker (13)
**3.** Notion (4)
**4.** Jumpers, cardigans, for example (8)
**5.** Excessively desirous of success (4,9)
**6.** Actor's lines (6)
**12.** Bearded (8)
**15.** Without usual standards or principles (6)
**17.** Disregard (6)
**19.** Organ of smell (4)

**solution on page 195**                                                      81

# Puzzle 78

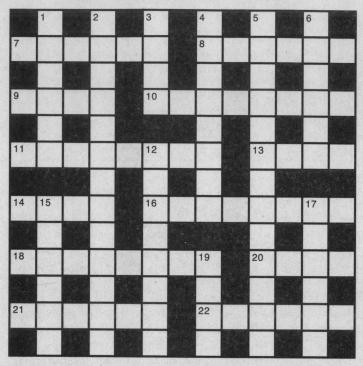

## Across

7. Package (6)
8. Most lazy (6)
9. Indian dress (4)
10. Simplest structural unit of an element (8)
11. Becoming very cold and icy (8)
13. Insensitive (4)
14. Make changes in text (4)
16. Pre-dinner drink (8)
18. Storyteller (8)
20. Alleviate (4)
21. Island to the north of Java (6)
22. Fortified wine (6)

## Down

1. Market-place (6)
2. Inclined to suffer mishaps (8-5)
3. Sullen (4)
4. Conversation between two persons (8)
5. Imprudent (3-10)
6. Sanctuary (6)
12. State of motionlessness (8)
15. Mythical fire-breather (6)
17. Put in (6)
19. Level to the ground (4)

solution on page 195

# Puzzle 79

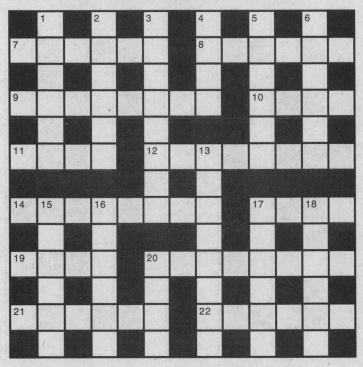

## Across

**7.** Well-being (6)
**8.** Alternative—this or that (6)
**9.** Extinct reptile (8)
**10.** Not at home (4)
**11.** Tidings (4)
**12.** Blinked (8)
**14.** Amazing occurrences (8)
**17.** Prayer ending word (4)
**19.** Precious metal (4)
**20.** Marauder (8)
**21.** Vocation (6)
**22.** Dozen (6)

## Down

**1.** Make up one's mind (6)
**2.** Blossoms (6)
**3.** Missile filled with oddments (8)
**4.** Carry (4)
**5.** Canadian capital (6)
**6.** Woman (6)
**13.** Music tape (8)
**15.** Pressure line on weather map (6)
**16.** Patron saint of Scotland (6)
**17.** Rhododendron-like shrub (6)
**18.** Develop (6)
**20.** Left side of ship (4)

solution on page 196

# Puzzle 80

## Across

1. Cherry brandy (6)
4. North African desert (6)
7. Spotted wildcat (6)
9. Not in good health (4)
11. Rodent (3)
12. Capital of Norway (4)
13. Boiler (6)
14. Take exception to (5)
16. Secure (4)
17. Tussock (4)
18. Juliet's partner (5)
21. Imaginary place considered perfect (6)
23. Too (4)
25. Pose (3)
26. Wheel shaft (4)
27. Archeological relic (6)
29. Offensively bold (6)
30. Zodiacal sign (6)

## Down

1. Booth (5)
2. Repent (3)
3. Repugnance (6)
4. Arrangement (6)
5. Enquires (4)
6. Agile performer (7)
8. Compartment for post (6-3)
10. Gracious (9)
15. Stretch (3)
16. Diabolical (7)
19. Wretchedness (6)
20. Kit (6)
22. Book of maps (5)
24. Mentally healthy (4)
28. Form of address (3)

solution on page 196

# Puzzle 81

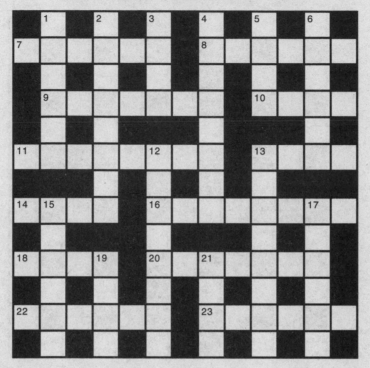

## Across

7. Theatrical dance routine (6)
8. Pressure line on weather map (6)
9. Most merciful (7)
10. Delayed (4)
11. Posture (8)
13. Went down (4)
14. Garden pest (4)
16. Breathing out (8)
18. Stare at (4)
20. Fiasco (7)
22. River that flows into the Dead Sea (6)
23. Snuggle (6)

## Down

1. Small and often ornate box for holding valuables (6)
2. Intermingling (8)
3. Eye infection (4)
4. Two per cent, as a fraction (8)
5. Seethe (4)
6. Administrative division of a country, e.g. Switzerland (6)
12. Continuing forever (8)
13. Socially awkward or tactless act (8)
15. Body of water cut off by a reef of sand or coral (6)
17. Pine leaf (6)
19. Whirlpool (4)
21. Stripe of contrasting color (4)

**solution on page 196**

# Puzzle 82

## Across

1. Cured herring (6)
4. Ladder-steps (5)
8. Fable writer (5)
9. Russian tea urn (7)
10. Charm (British, 7)
11. Pastry case (4)
12. Japanese currency (3)
14. Military cap (4)
15. Minor prophet (4)
18. Tune (3)
21. Eastern staple food (4)
23. Vaulted passage (7)
25. Commercial stoppage (7)
26. Garden bush (5)
27. Sycophant (5)
28. Glitter (6)

## Down

1. Jacks in a playing card pack (6)
2. Corridor (7)
3. Jubilation (8)
4. Gambol (4)
5. Fictional work (5)
6. Malay garment (6)
7. Excessive interest (5)
13. Spring flowers (8)
16. Forwards (7)
17. Religious leader (6)
19. Shaving tool (5)
20. Percussion instrument (6)
22. Venomous snake (5)
24. Wild party involving excessive drinking and promiscuity (4)

# Puzzle 83

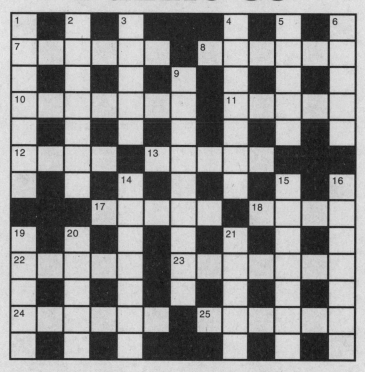

## Across

7. Peculiar person (6)
8. Fit for cultivation (6)
10. Element (7)
11. Luster (5)
12. Pay increase (4)
13. Imitation (5)
17. Presents (5)
18. God of Thunder (4)
22. Large ape (5)
23. Greek mountain (7)
24. Large gun (6)
25. Positive particle (6)

## Down

1. Milk food (7)
2. Worship (British, 7)
3. Platform (5)
4. Tedious (7)
5. Receded (5)
6. Unit of currency (5)
9. Sixth sense (9)
14. Freshwater duck (7)
15. Indian bread (7)
16. Blotting out (7)
19. Dog (5)
20. Child's nurse (5)
21. Spa (5)

# Puzzle 84

## Across

1. Striped animal (5)
4. Indian washerman (5)
10. Potion dispenser (7)
11. Solitary (5)
12. Scavenging carnivore (5)
13. Recreation (7)
15. Biblical garden (4)
17. Garden flower (5)
19. Friendly Islands (5)
22. Animal's den (4)
25. Stimulate (7)
27. Sofa (5)
29. Suburban residences (5)
30. Run away (slang) (7)
31. Huge sea (5)
32. Decorate (5)

## Down

2. Wear away (5)
3. Renaissance painter (7)
5. Piles (5)
6. Reservation (7)
7. State of NW America (5)
8. Fumble (5)
9. Units of heredity (5)
14. Opposed (4)
16. Valley (4)
18. Muslim (7)
20. Fruit garden (7)
21. Irritate (5)
23. Acute remorse (5)
24. Fleeced (5)
26. Scene (5)
28. Superior (5)

solution on page 197

# Puzzle 85

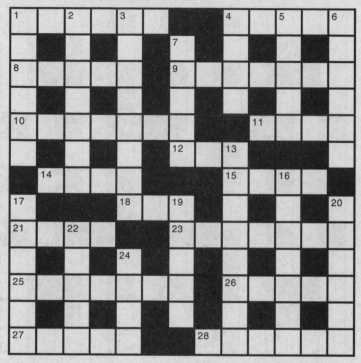

## Across

1. Seafarer (6)
4. Office worker (5)
8. Successfully potted (5)
9. Esteemed (7)
10. Bemoans (7)
11. Hint (4)
12. Fuss (3)
14. Plan (4)
15. Canine cry (4)
18. Rider Haggard novel (3)
21. Vagrant (4)
23. Most direct route (7)
25. Iranian (7)
26. Human utterance (5)
27. Female relative (5)
28. Fabulous monster (6)

## Down

1. African desert (6)
2. Prohibited (7)
3. Remnants (8)
4. Unconscious state (4)
5. Register (5)
6. Renal organ (6)
7. Light wood (5)
13. Watcher (8)
16. Lifting (7)
17. Polish composer (6)
19. Black wood (5)
20. Belittle (6)
22. Canal boat (5)
24. Calamitous (4)

# Puzzle 86

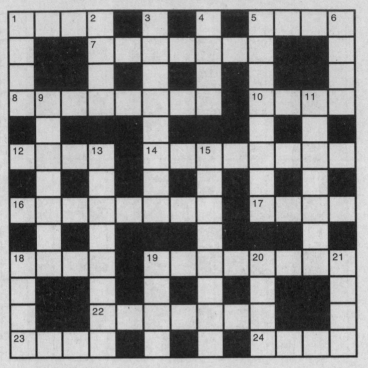

## Across

1. Change course (4)
5. Circle (4)
7. Bill (7)
8. Ragged (8)
10. Money (4)
12. Detect (4)
14. Enthralling (8)
16. Without equal (8)
17. Boy's name (4)
18. Norwegian city (4)
19. Believable (8)
22. Treachery (7)
23. Engrave (4)
24. Put in order (4)

## Down

1. Underwear (4)
2. Uproar (4)
3. Set aside (8)
4. Genial (4)
5. Response (8)
6. Spout (4)
9. Replies (7)
11. Exceptional (7)
13. Isle of Wight resort (8)
15. Apprehension about what's going to happen (8)
18. Seep (4)
19. Ship's company (4)
20. Charged particles (4)
21. Give forth (4)

solution on page 198

# Puzzle 87

## Across

7. Notice for sale (6)
8. Interior (6)
10. Transgression (7)
11. Come into flower (5)
12. Fish (4)
13. Started (5)
17. Military dictators (5)
18. Retain (4)
22. Digit (5)
23. Free from blame (7)
24. Beverage (6)
25. Calm (6)

## Down

1. Balearic island (7)
2. Egg-shaped (7)
3. Fetch (5)
4. Aardvark (7)
5. Prejudiced person (5)
6. Smiles with pleasure (5)
9. Heavenly (9)
14. Effervesced (7)
15. Marriage (7)
16. Adds something extra (7)
19. Pile (5)
20. Collars (5)
21. Devotional song (5)

# Puzzle 88

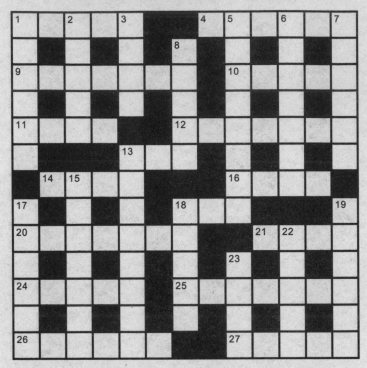

## Across

1. Ventriloquist's prop (5)
4. People in a play (6)
9. Collection of books (7)
10. Over the top (5)
11. Spindle (4)
12. Accuse of treason (7)
13. Legendary bird (3)
14. Musical instrument (4)
16. Devastate (slang) (4)
18. Domestic parasite (3)
20. Laugh quietly (7)
21. Doorpost (4)
24. Framework (5)
25. Artlessness (7)
26. Outlet (6)
27. Quoted (5)

## Down

1. Texan city (6)
2. Woman's name (5)
3. Twelve months (4)
5. Hacking (8)
6. Australia's bush (7)
7. Boil (6)
8. Sarcastic pessimist (5)
13. Rash (8)
15. Mistake (7)
17. Frozen spike (6)
18. Vegetables (5)
19. Complied (6)
22. Vigilant (5)
23. Metallic element (4)

solution on page 199

# Puzzle 89

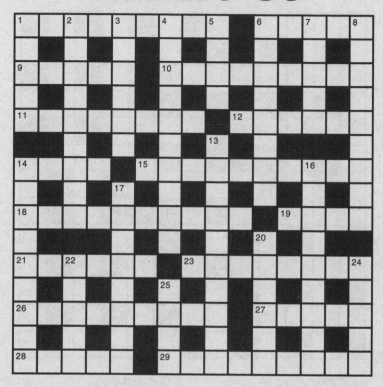

The answers in this crossword are anagrams of their clues, but can you discover the correct anagram in every case? (For instance, the solution to a clue such as 'Adder' could be either 'Dared' or 'Dread'... the choice isn't always obvious!)

## Across

1. Rue beagle (9)
6. Mob ma (5)
9. Mad go (5)
10. Gilt genie (9)
11. Mud chant (8)
12. Sec sac (6)
14. Tory (4)
15. Invited oar (10)
18. Ugly armlet (10)
19. Prey (4)
21. I learn (6)
23. Hep fells (4-4)
26. Prior pout (9)
27. To gin (5)
28. A seed (5)
29. Erg veneer (9)

## Down

1. Be odd (5)
2. Shot guilt (6,3)
3. Pat hay (6)
4. Careful gnu (10)
5. Lyre (4)
6. Gain mica (8)
7. Me or I (5)
8. Bee casino (9)
13. Eel filings (6,4)
14. Impale set (4-5)
16. I gave Yule (3,6)
17. Koala lid (8)
20. Fin fog (6)
22. Stone (5)
24. At pen (5)
25. Reef (4)

# Puzzle 90

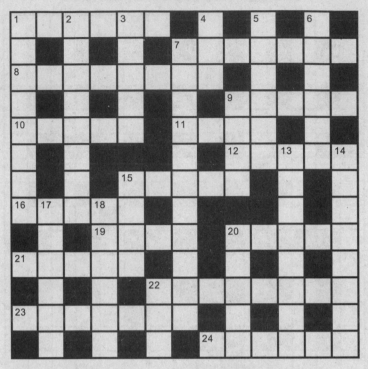

## Across

1. Mob (6)
7. Cruel killer (7)
8. Swamp (8)
9. Underground worker (5)
10. Gold block (5)
11. Handle (4)
12. Moderately warm (5)
15. Thump (5)
16. Simple song (5)
19. Egg on (4)
20. Lose consciousness (5)
21. Distress signal (5)
22. Break bone (8)
23. Occupy (7)
24. Strain (6)

## Down

1. Needed (8)
2. Boaster (8)
3. Extent (5)
4. Complexion (3)
5. Old copyist (6)
6. Middle Easterner (6)
7. Sign of great unhappiness (6,5)
9. Flying insect (4)
13. Foot care (8)
14. Dexterity (8)
15. Funeral pile (4)
17. Sea-girt territory (6)
18. Sikh headdress (6)
20. Slant or surface (5)
22. Tree (3)

solution on page 199

# Puzzle 91

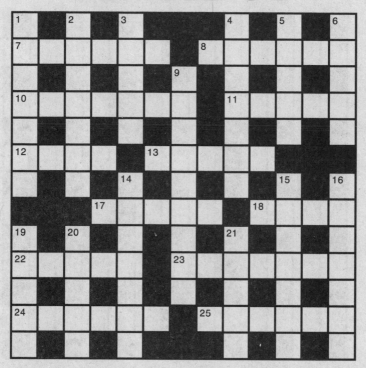

## Across

7. Man's name (6)
8. Senility (6)
10. Generosity (7)
11. Summit (5)
12. The price (4)
13. Confronted (5)
17. Refuse to go on (British, 5)
18. Asked (4)
22. Line up (5)
23. Pouch on kilt (7)
24. Paper handkerchief (6)
25. Money man (6)

## Down

1. Poisonous plant (7)
2. Form a hard coating (7)
3. Cinema attendant (5)
4. Receipt (7)
5. Avid (5)
6. Irish poet (5)
9. Set up (9)
14. Paper-reed (7)
15. Capsicum spice (7)
16. Church house (7)
19. Artificial gems (5)
20. Quick and energetic (5)
21. Ethical (5)

**solution on page 200**

# Puzzle 92

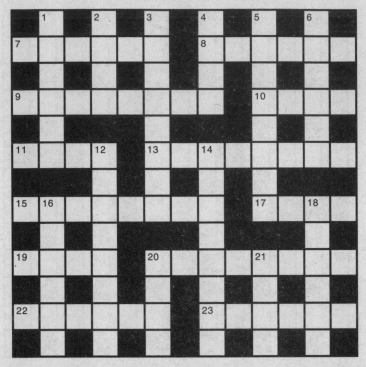

## Across

**7.** Appetizer, usually consisting of bread spread with a savory (6)

**8.** Hairstylist (6)

**9.** Any liquid suitable for drinking (8)

**10.** Kinship group (4)

**11.** Vessel for travel on water (4)

**13.** Renounce the throne (8)

**15.** Withers (8)

**17.** Facilitate (4)

**19.** Suggestion (4)

**20.** Mediterranean island west of Italy (8)

**22.** Food prepared from the pressed curd of milk (6)

**23.** Singe (6)

## Down

**1.** Summer-house (6)

**2.** Completely unclothed (4)

**3.** Come apart (8)

**4.** Capable (4)

**5.** Three-wheeled bike (8)

**6.** Pour wine or sherry into decorative container (6)

**12.** "Unlucky" number (8)

**14.** Psychological suffering (8)

**16.** Vertical dimension (6)

**18.** Interchange (6)

**20.** Look for (4)

**21.** Metal which readily rusts (4)

solution on page 200

# Puzzle 93

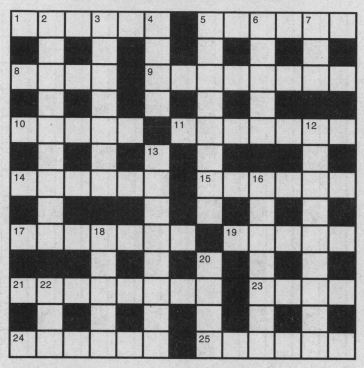

## Across

1. Toil (British, 6)
5. Pleasantly occupied (6)
8. Eye infection (4)
9. American car (8)
10. Strong and sharp (5)
11. Rapture (7)
14. Volatile (6)
15. Maneuver (6)
17. Versus (7)
19. Noisy fight (5)
21. Astound (8)
23. Region (4)
24. Catalyst (6)
25. Offensively bold (6)

## Down

2. Fastening together (9)
3. Tapering stone pillar (7)
4. Contest of speed (4)
5. Give up throne (8)
6. Dark (5)
7. Time period (3)
12. Sunken vessel (9)
13. Sweat (8)
16. Butchery (7)
18. Satire (5)
20. Stylish (4)
22. Male offspring (3)

solution on page 200

# Puzzle 94

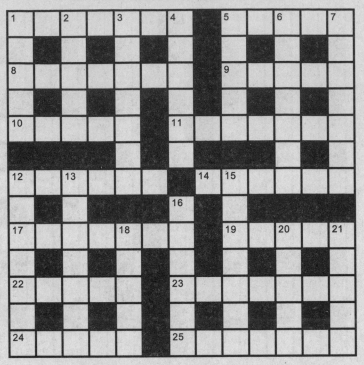

## Across

1. Fail to meet financial obligation (7)
5. Accolade (5)
8. Shoemaker (7)
9. Dramas (5)
10. Military blockade (5)
11. Gap (7)
12. Wallops (6)
14. Estimates (6)
17. Liquidizer (7)
19. Very fast (5)
22. Cognizant, awake to what is happening (5)
23. Cleanliness (7)
24. Put pressure on (5)
25. Went around (7)

## Down

1. Evades (5)
2. Legend (5)
3. Most unsightly (7)
4. Overwhelming fear (6)
5. Common fruit (5)
6. Astounding (7)
7. Patterns (7)
12. Garden vegetable (7)
13. Control (7)
15. Vertical (7)
16. Bowman (6)
18. Inhabited (5)
20. Pressed fold (5)
21. Apprehension (5)

 solution on page 201

# Puzzle 95

## Across

1. Desolate (7)
4. Foundation (5)
7. Wireless (5)
10. Large artery (5)
11. Truck with an enclosed cargo space (3)
12. Feline mammal (3)
13. Ooze (5)
14. Writing implement (5)
16. Residential district, often rundown (6)
18. Inconsistent in quality (6)
22. Punctuation mark (5)
24. Cleave (5)
26. Extinct flightless bird of New Zealand (3)
27. Quarry (3)
28. Illusion (5)
29. Bread-raising agent (5)
31. Cards used for fortune telling (5)
32. Number (7)

## Down

1. Powerful effect or influence (5)
2. Ornamental garland (3)
3. Subtle difference in meaning (6)
4. Mountainous republic in southeastern Asia (5)
5. Crude dwelling (5)
6. Division (7)
8. The two in a pack of playing cards (5)
9. Open (5)
15. Side sheltered from wind (3)
16. Article of clothing (7)
17. Likewise (3)
19. Offensive (5)
20. Country house (5)
21. Serviette made of cloth (6)
22. Supply (5)
23. Slightly wet (5)
25. Entire (5)
30. Stretch (3)

solution on page 201

# Puzzle 96

## Across

2. Emblem (5)
5. Lessen (5)
8. Fuss (3)
9. Variety of peach (9)
11. Bare (5)
12. Seriously (9)
15. Approval (6)
16. Quarters for military personnel (6)
18. Accused party (9)
21. Enroll (5)
22. Policeman's club (9)
24. Tub (3)
25. Allow in (5)
26. Panorama (5)

## Down

1. Coloring medium (5)
2. Place to keep novels (9)
3. Common weed (9)
4. Bodyguard (6)
6. Sets on fire (5)
7. Light brown (3)
10. N African country (5)
13. Being (9)
14. Loquacious (9)
15. Military trainee (5)
17. Stroke tenderly (6)
19. Tedium (5)
20. Thin, meat soup (5)
23. Relieve from (3)

solution on page 201

# Puzzle 97

## Across

1. Package (6)
4. Savory flan (6)
9. Violent disorder (7)
10. Detests (5)
11. Fashion (5)
12. Slaughter (7)
13. Make free from confusion (British, 11)
18. Snapped (7)
20. Male relative (5)
22. Spare (5)
23. Makes unhappy (7)
24. Howl (6)
25. Shortsightedness (6)

## Down

1. Examine (6)
2. Card game (5)
3. Pencil rubbers (7)
5. Doorkeeper (5)
6. Short, curved sword (7)
7. Resulted (6)
8. Wares (11)
14. Nuclear plant (7)
15. Washing (7)
16. Admittance (6)
17. Iran, formerly (6)
19. Australian bear (5)
21. Inexpensive (5)

solution on page 202

# Puzzle 98

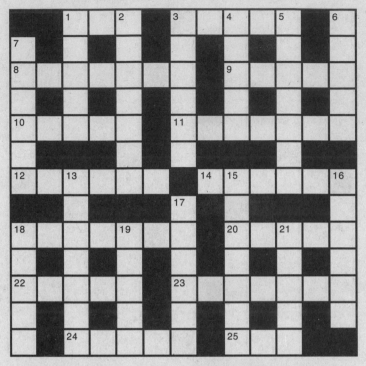

## Across

1. Took a seat (3)
3. Bear, convey (5)
8. Recant (7)
9. Bohemian dance (5)
10. Tree, emblem of Canada (5)
11. Loosening the ties (7)
12. Objective (6)
14. Solid lump of a precious metal (6)
18. Having the requisite qualities for (7)
20. Receive (5)
22. Survive (5)
23. Strong feeling (7)
24. Foe (5)
25. Adult male person (3)

## Down

1. Assemble (3,2)
2. Swing used by circus acrobats (7)
3. Juicy fruit, such as lemon, orange, etc (6)
4. Very fast (5)
5. Howling (7)
6. Jargon (5)
7. On time (6)
13. Cold-blooded vertebrate (7)
15. Consistent (7)
16. Monarch's seat (6)
17. Salad vegetable (6)
18. Sneak (5)
19. Swim or wash (5)
21. Mound of stones piled up as a memorial (5)

**solution on page 202**

# Puzzle 99

## Across

1. Close at hand (6)
4. Large monkey with dog-like muzzle (6)
8. Filth (5)
10. Short high tone (5)
11. Absolutely necessary (5)
12. Banal (5)
14. Boredom (5)
16. Club (3)
18. Company emblem (4)
19. Very dry (4)
21. Shake (3)
24. Native American tent (5)
27. Sweet sticky liquid (5)
29. Bingo (5)
30. Goodbye (5)
31. Backslide (5)
32. Large, edible bird (6)
33. Supplication (6)

## Down

1. Contravene (6)
2. Self-justification (5)
3. Mark placed over a vowel to indicate a short sound (5)
5. Saunter (5)
6. Large body of water (5)
7. Serviette made of cloth (6)
9. Sicilian volcano (4)
13. Relating to them (5)
15. Loud (5)
16. Knot with two loops and loose ends (3)
17. Children's game (3)
20. Narrow channel of the sea (6)
22. Lowest female singing voice (4)
23. Seem (6)
25. Earlier in time (5)
26. Evade (5)
27. Of the sun (5)
28. Forming viscous or glutinous threads (5)

solution on page 202

# Puzzle 100

## Across

2. Burn with steam (5)
4. Timber that is floating or has been washed ashore (9)
6. Mythical being, son of Daedalus (6)
8. Delilah's partner (6)
10. Pick off (5)
11. Bonfire signal (6)
12. Cut with teeth (6)
13. Glances over (5)
15. Popular beverage (6)
16. Incumbency (6)
18. County in northern England, divided into three parts (9)
19. Belonging to them (5)

## Down

1. Well-being (6)
2. Make an error (4,2)
3. Antonin ——, Czech composer (1841–1904) (6)
4. Slender-bodied non-stinging insect (9)
5. Deface (9)
6. Old Testament patriarch (5)
7. Cut into pieces (5)
8. Limited in quality or quantity (5)
9. Saltpeter (British, 5)
13. Clandestine (6)
14. Higher in rank (6)
17. Slumbering (6)

solution on page 203

# Puzzle 101

## Across

1. Country (6)
4. Sample (3,3)
7. Spaceman (9)
9. Penultimate Greek letter (3)
10. Donkey (3)
11. Jump on one foot (3)
14. Rivulet (4)
15. Self-indulgent idlers (8)
17. Native American tent (5)
18. Fell down like a waterfall (8)
19. Horny foot (4)
21. Piece of scrap material (3)
22. Slippery fish (3)
24. Crazy (3)
25. Christmasses (9)
28. Reward (6)
29. Go by (6)

## Down

1. Pincer (6)
2. —— and outs (3)
3. Tapered (8)
4. Marine fish (4)
5. Not me (3)
6. Convolutes (6)
7. Without purpose (9)
8. Intestinal parasites (9)
12. Writing material (5)
13. Consumed (3)
16. Tranquilizer (8)
17. Faucet (3)
18. Angel (6)
20. Violin (6)
23. Resist (4)
26. Pot (3)
27. Mrs Sharples of Coronation Street fame (3)

# Puzzle 102

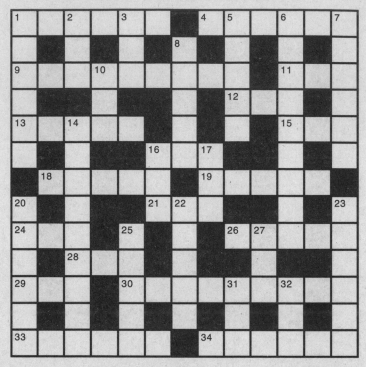

## Across

1. Show submission or fear (6)
4. Lustrous (6)
9. Swayed towards a course of action (9)
11. Sick (3)
12. Liquor flavored with juniper berries (3)
13. Commonly encountered (5)
15. Self-importance (3)
16. As well as (3)
18. Coral reef (5)
19. Run off to wed (5)
21. Rules imposed by authority (3)
24. Intent (3)
26. Start (5)
28. Atmosphere (3)
29. Shack (3)
30. Form of transport (British, 9)
33. Smile affectedly (6)
34. Musical composition written for six performers (6)

## Down

1. Common white or colorless mineral (6)
2. Paddle (3)
3. Flightless bird (3)
5. Long raised strip (5)
6. Domesticated cavy (6-3)
7. Candle ingredient (6)
8. Embellish (5)
10. Health resort (3)
14. Final peremptory demand (9)
16. Whole (3)
17. Overnight condensation (3)
20. Commiseration (6)
22. Terminate (5)
23. Taint (6)
25. Couple (5)
27. Slippery fish (3)
31. Pastry dish (3)
32. Behave (3)

solution on page 203

# Puzzle 103

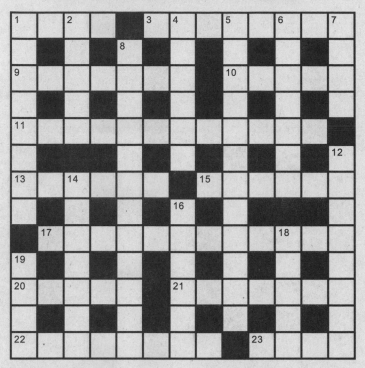

## Across

**1.** See (4)
**3.** Merry-go-round (8)
**9.** Bridge (7)
**10.** Of the sun (5)
**11.** In close proximity (British, 12)
**13.** Expensive white fur (6)
**15.** Intrigue (6)
**17.** Unnaturally (12)
**20.** Self-justification (5)
**21.** Clinging part of plant (7)
**22.** Three-wheeled bike (8)
**23.** Unwanted plant (4)

## Down

**1.** Aromatic shrub (8)
**2.** Giraffe-like creature (5)
**4.** Something done (6)
**5.** Obstacles (12)
**6.** To quiet (7)
**7.** Hang around (4)
**8.** Legitimacy (12)
**12.** Reprocessed (8)
**14.** Cocktail (7)
**16.** Beam over doorway (6)
**18.** Big (5)
**19.** Lure (4)

solution on page 204

# Puzzle 104

## Across

1. Machine tool (5)
4. Three score and ten (7)
7. Self-justification (5)
8. South American rodent resembling a small beaver (5)
10. Religious woman (3)
11. Sound made by dove (3)
12. Eskimo's canoe (5)
14. Jangle, clash (5)
15. Color of the rainbow (6)
18. Large bottle of Champagne (6)
22. Spiritual leader (5)
23. Animal (5)
26. By way of (3)
27. Employ (3)
28. Lessen (5)
30. Peak (5)
31. Reins (7)
32. Unclean (5)

## Down

1. Washing (7)
2. Express gratitude (5)
3. Enlighten (5)
4. Glutinous (6)
5. Inflated pride (3)
6. In an early period of life (5)
8. Chocolate powder (5)
9. Languish (5)
13. Sicken (3)
16. Sign of the zodiac (5)
17. Cocktail fruit (5)
19. Oxygen, for instance (3)
20. Freedom from vanity (7)
21. Counting frame (6)
22. Get to (5)
24. In front of (5)
25. Coach (5)
29. Light brown (3)

solution on page 204

# Puzzle 105

## Across

**1.** Small cask (3)
**3.** Intense burst of radiant energy (5)
**8.** Stringed instrument (5)
**9.** Enraged (7)
**10.** Stomach (7)
**11.** Obvious and dull (5)
**12.** Amount (6)
**14.** Signboard, for example, bearing shopkeeper's name (6)
**18.** Small and elegant (5)
**20.** Day of rest and worship (7)
**22.** Analgesic substance (7)
**23.** Fertile tract in desert (5)
**24.** Fearful expectation (5)
**25.** Twitch (3)

## Down

**1.** Realm (7)
**2.** Atmosphere of depression (5)
**3.** Show off (6)
**4.** Branch of mathematics (7)
**5.** Wading bird (5)
**6.** Foot-lever (5)
**7.** Get (6)
**13.** Learned (7)
**15.** Creation of the highest excellence (7)
**16.** Appalled (6)
**17.** Go up (6)
**18.** Slice of pig's meat (5)
**19.** Fatigued (5)
**21.** Encourage (5)

solution on page 204

# Puzzle 106

## Across

1. Precious gem (7)
5. Cavalry sword (5)
8. Guides (5)
9. Ninepin (7)
10. Time period (3)
11. Persistently continual (9)
13. Rite (6)
14. Went without food (6)
17. Misery resulting from affliction (9)
19. Chest bone (3)
21. Transform from a useless or uncultivated state (7)
23. Test (5)
24. Go in (5)
25. Pitched (7)

## Down

1. Dig deeply into (5)
2. Unsusceptible to persuasion (7)
3. Stubborn (9)
4. Refrain (6)
5. Travel across snow (3)
6. Swim or wash (5)
7. Made a great effort (7)
12. Carnage (9)
13. Earmark (7)
15. Sully (7)
16. Gloomy (6)
18. Aspect (5)
20. Pulled in, bundled (5)
22. Melody (3)

solution on page 205

# Puzzle 107

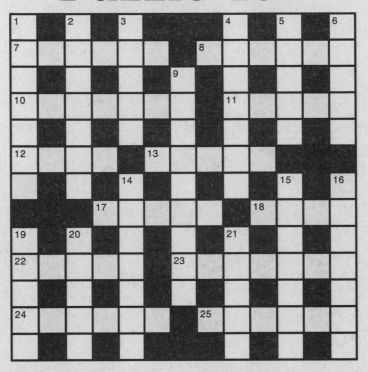

## Across

**7.** Mob (6)
**8.** Keen (6)
**10.** Mobile holiday home (7)
**11.** Arabian spirit (5)
**12.** Medium-length dress (4)
**13.** Main artery (5)
**17.** Operatic airs (5)
**18.** Commotion (4)
**22.** Cinders (5)
**23.** Floor show (7)
**24.** Mission (6)
**25.** Sharp-eyed birds (6)

## Down

**1.** Greek money (7)
**2.** Push in (7)
**3.** Pungent spice (5)
**4.** Warship (7)
**5.** Large flower (5)
**6.** Guide vessel (5)
**9.** Chagrin (9)
**14.** Gift (7)
**15.** Frighten (7)
**16.** Complain (7)
**19.** Desert animal (5)
**20.** Allure (5)
**21.** Submarine (1-4)

solution on page 205

# Puzzle 108

## Across

**1.** Surging (7)
**5.** Food made from dough of flour or meal (5)
**8.** Preliminary sketch of a design (5)
**9.** Poorly balanced or matched in quantity (7)
**10.** Ugly, evil-looking old woman (3)
**11.** Saying that is widely accepted on its own merits (5)
**12.** Put out or expelled (7)
**14.** Wallcovering (11)
**20.** Cause to be amazed (7)
**23.** Picture puzzle (5)
**25.** Large deer (3)
**26.** Inaccurate (7)
**27.** Audacious (5)
**28.** Herb (5)
**29.** Return to a former state (7)

## Down

**1.** Astrological region of constellations (6)
**2.** Giraffe-like creature (5)
**3.** Narrow strip of land (with water on both sides) connecting two larger land areas (7)
**4.** Estimate (5)
**5.** Mark placed over a vowel to indicate a short sound (5)
**6.** Imaginary line round the Earth (7)
**7.** Lead on (6)
**13.** Shock physically (3)
**15.** Gamble, game of chance (7)
**16.** Light brown (3)
**17.** Container for sewing tools (7)
**18.** Lasso (6)
**19.** Evaluate (6)
**21.** Accepted practice (5)
**22.** Dissuade (5)
**24.** Sharp part of knife (5)

**solution on page 205**

# Puzzle 109

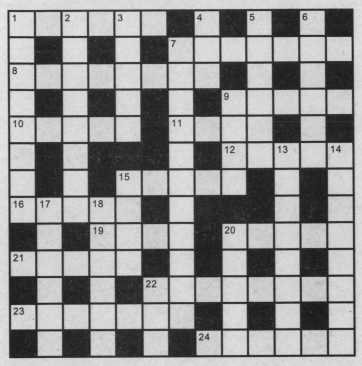

## Across

1. Insignificant (6)
7. Colonist (7)
8. Totaling (8)
9. Envy (5)
10. Roman river (5)
11. God of thunder (4)
12. Curved sword (5)
15. Aromatic resin (5)
16. First name of racing driver Irvine (5)
19. Body of the church (4)
20. Dilate (5)
21. Summit (5)
22. Kiss (8)
23. Break up (7)
24. Metal ring for lining a small hole, most commonly in fabric (6)

## Down

1. Professional business (8)
2. Insect (8)
3. Helicopter propeller (5)
4. Serious offence (3)
5. Mohair (6)
6. Decorative layer (6)
7. Troublesome ghost (11)
9. Bludgeon (4)
13. US national game (8)
14. Outflow (8)
15. Flesh used as food (4)
17. Famous naturalist (6)
18. Put in (6)
20. Cheeky (5)
22. Choose (3)

solution on page 206

# Puzzle 110

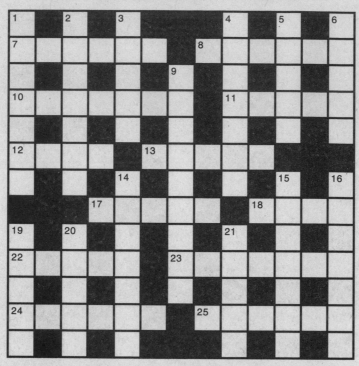

## Across

**7.** Bird house (6)
**8.** Detest (6)
**10.** Line touching curve (7)
**11.** Ingrained dirt (5)
**12.** Cloud (4)
**13.** Breadmaker (5)
**17.** Measuring instrument (5)
**18.** Disjoin (4)
**22.** Vigilant (5)
**23.** Commercial stoppage (7)
**24.** Mark of infamy (6)
**25.** Declare (6)

## Down

**1.** Music of the 30s (7)
**2.** Keyboard player (7)
**3.** Angler's basket (5)
**4.** Cross-breed (7)
**5.** Garret (5)
**6.** Cleave (5)
**9.** Notorious Boston murderer (9)
**14.** Hobby (7)
**15.** Knotty (7)
**16.** Capital of Ontario (7)
**19.** Fall out of date (5)
**20.** Great danger (5)
**21.** Treat badly (5)

solution on page 206

# Puzzle 111

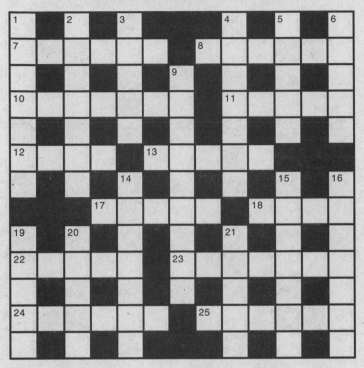

## Across

**7.** Rifled (6)
**8.** Fuss (6)
**10.** Hearing distance (7)
**11.** Elevates (5)
**12.** Dry biscuit (4)
**13.** Shine (5)
**17.** Lawbreaking (5)
**18.** Substantive (4)
**22.** Australian city (5)
**23.** Embryonic frog (7)
**24.** Dried grape (6)
**25.** Senior nurse (6)

## Down

**1.** Mathematical system (7)
**2.** Feed (7)
**3.** Indian city (5)
**4.** Rich stew (7)
**5.** Robbery (5)
**6.** Hand joint (5)
**9.** Deadlock (9)
**14.** Antiquated (7)
**15.** Stay (7)
**16.** Horrific fire (7)
**19.** Snub (5)
**20.** Characteristic (5)
**21.** Perfect model (5)

solution on page 206

# Puzzle 112

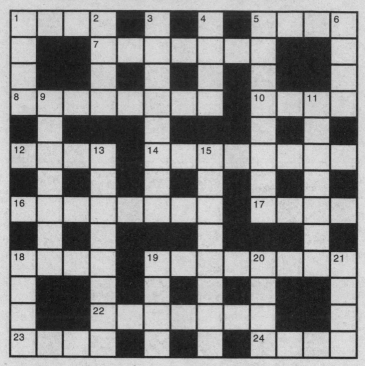

## Across

1. Distort (4)
5. Individual unit (4)
7. Forsake (7)
8. Breed of cattle (8)
10. Swirl (4)
12. Speck of soot (4)
14. Maritime (8)
16. Looking gloomy (8)
17. Tatters (4)
18. Supplication (4)
19. Entire (8)
22. Remain longer than necessary (7)
23. Secure a ship (4)
24. Kill (4)

## Down

1. Homeless orphan (4)
2. Head (4)
3. Ranch (8)
4. Norse deity (4)
5. Inside (8)
6. Numerous (4)
9. Transference (7)
11. Current of air (7)
13. Bullfighter (8)
15. Utmost (8)
18. Tropical tree (4)
19. Daintily pretty (4)
20. Deposits (4)
21. Jumpy (4)

solution on page 207

# Puzzle 113

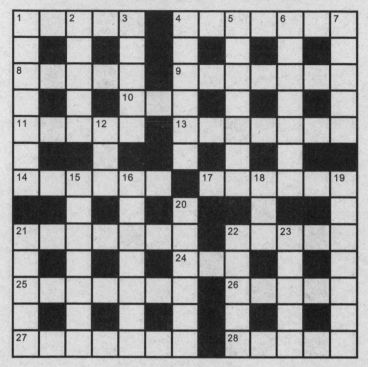

## Across

**1.** Out of practice (5)
**4.** Watch attentively (7)
**8.** South American rodent resembling a small beaver (5)
**9.** Spear thrown in field events (7)
**10.** Golfing device (3)
**11.** Native to Eire (5)
**13.** Bravery (7)
**14.** Solution used for rinsing the mouth (6)
**17.** Fire-breathing dragon used in medieval heraldry (6)
**21.** Shoulder blade (7)
**22.** Overzealous (5)
**24.** Named prior to marriage (3)
**25.** Regular payment (7)
**26.** Infectious agent (5)
**27.** Typographical error (7)
**28.** Egyptian water lily (5)

## Down

**1.** Swaying (7)
**2.** Record player needles (5)
**3.** Juvenility (5)
**4.** Target (6)
**5.** Having an agreeably pungent taste (British, 7)
**6.** Discharge (7)
**7.** Forename of S African golfer Els (5)
**12.** Settle from pressure or loss of tautness (3)
**15.** More prepared (7)
**16.** Greatest in volume (7)
**18.** By way of (3)
**19.** Naturists (7)
**20.** Bicycle for two riders (6)
**21.** Little Susan (5)
**22.** Make merry (5)
**23.** Fired (5)

solution on page 207

# Puzzle 114

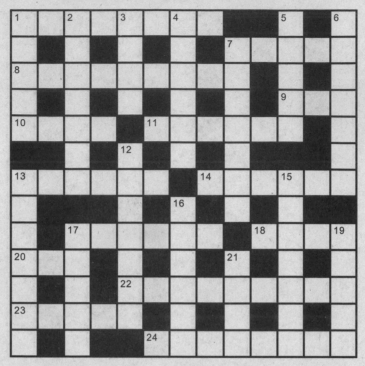

## Across

**1.** Fire-raiser (8)
**7.** Identification tab (5)
**8.** Russian musical instrument (9)
**9.** Artful (3)
**10.** Heroic (4)
**11.** Posture (6)
**13.** Fine building stone (6)
**14.** Guiding light (6)
**17.** Break through (6)
**18.** Operatic solo (4)
**20.** Constricting snake (3)
**22.** Former citizen of Zimbabwe (9)
**23.** Cuban dance (5)
**24.** Denoting cultural traditions (8)

## Down

**1.** Easy pace (5)
**2.** Fighter (7)
**3.** African river (4)
**4.** Walking poles (6)
**5.** Abnormally fat (5)
**6.** Baby's recreation area (7)
**7.** Wash clothes (7)
**12.** Mathematical system (7)
**13.** Those who belong (7)
**15.** Of the heart (7)
**16.** Confront (6)
**17.** Mild and pleasant weather (5)
**19.** Make void (5)
**21.** Rare gas (4)

solution on page 207

# Puzzle 115

## Across

1. Cobbler's stand (4)
3. Penned (8)
9. Short high tone (5)
10. Spiced Spanish wine (7)
11. Auction item (3)
13. A gradual increase in volume (9)
14. Group of words (6)
16. Spiritually converted (6)
18. Languor (9)
20. Fixed (3)
22. Absorbent paper used to dry or mop up excessive ink (7)
23. A lengthwise crack in wood (5)
25. Infinite time (8)
26. Fuel item (4)

## Down

1. Written slander (5)
2. Girl's name (3)
4. Shellfish often considered an aphrodisiac (6)
5. Flair (7)
6. Very difficult and demanding much energy (9)
7. Compel by threatening (7)
8. Heroic (4)
12. Change the order or arrangement of something (9)
14. Degree of excellence or worth (British, 7)
15. Affected suddenly with deep feeling (7)
17. Small tower extending above a building (6)
19. Simple (4)
21. Entire (5)
24. Zodiacal lion (3)

# Puzzle 116

## Across

**2.** Utter confusion (5)
**4.** Heralded, widely praised (9)
**6.** Position (6)
**8.** Roof tiles (6)
**10.** Saline (5)
**11.** World-wide (6)
**12.** Fissure in the earth's crust (6)
**13.** Catapult (5)
**15.** Island in the Mediterranean (6)
**16.** Requiring less effort (6)
**18.** Power to withstand hardship or stress (9)
**19.** Vote (5)

## Down

**1.** Insect considered divine by ancient Egyptians (6)
**2.** Spine-bearing, succulent plant (6)
**3.** Without complication (6)
**4.** Slide of snow from mountainside (9)
**5.** Fix conclusively or authoritatively (9)
**6.** Items of footwear (5)
**7.** Unhappily (5)
**8.** Rock (5)
**9.** Forest god (5)
**13.** Any thick messy substance (6)
**14.** Semi-precious gemstone (6)
**17.** Gentle wind (6)

solution on page 208

# Puzzle 117

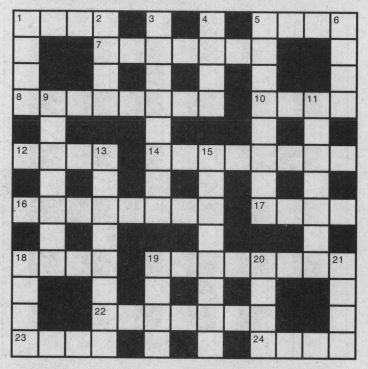

## Across

**1.** Interweave (4)
**5.** Curved gateway (4)
**7.** Local speech (7)
**8.** Block of flats (8)
**10.** Figure-skating jump (4)
**12.** Inflammation which can impair vision (4)
**14.** One who resists attacks (8)
**16.** Advocate of social equality (8)
**17.** Raised platform (4)
**18.** Found on a flower (4)
**19.** Report (8)
**22.** Tool (7)
**23.** Lodgings (4)
**24.** Alone (4)

## Down

**1.** Bewildered (4)
**2.** Boundary (4)
**3.** Record of annual dates (8)
**4.** Departed (4)
**5.** Achieved (8)
**6.** Cry of greeting (4)
**9.** Ask earnestly (7)
**11.** Former academics (7)
**13.** Huge (8)
**15.** One resigned to the inevitable (8)
**18.** Grains on the beach (4)
**19.** Bovine meat (4)
**20.** Long fish (4)
**21.** Roman emperor (4)

# Puzzle 118

## Across

1. Army rank (5)
4. Seller (6)
9. Tedious (7)
10. Conical tent (5)
11. Weird (4)
12. Conduct work (7)
13. Pastry (3)
14. Handle roughly (4)
16. Long journey (4)
18. Plaything (3)
20. Flair (7)
21. Cry in despair (4)
24. Aquatic mammal (5)
25. Misled (7)
26. Flee (6)
27. Basic drink (5)

## Down

1. Damsel (6)
2. Humorist (5)
3. Chessman (4)
5. Appeal (8)
6. Pervert (7)
7. Lurched (6)
8. English writer (5)
13. Plucking implement (8)
15. Related (7)
17. Maintain (6)
18. Fabric bear (5)
19. Motorless plane (6)
22. Check accounts (5)
23. Misfortune (4)

solution on page 209

# Puzzle 119

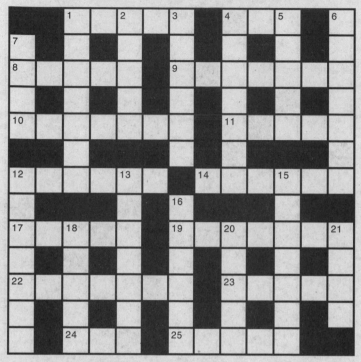

## Across

1. Jovial (5)
4. Add together (3)
8. Harden (5)
9. Stir up (7)
10. Hide (7)
11. Performing (5)
12. Alight (6)
14. After (6)
17. Scene of action (5)
19. Item of jewelry (7)
22. Standard or typical example (7)
23. Bore a hole (5)
24. Hydrogen, for instance (3)
25. Mythical, cave-dwelling creature (5)

## Down

1. Daybook (7)
2. Vassal (5)
3. Annually (6)
4. Rotating shaft (7)
5. Florida city (5)
6. Came out (7)
7. Phonograph record (4)
12. Learned institution (7)
13. Avid (7)
15. The first letter of a word (7)
16. Constituent of concrete (6)
18. Looking at (5)
20. Wireless (5)
21. Fete (4)

**solution on page 209**

# Puzzle 120

## Across

1. Apex (4)
3. Execution platform (8)
9. Courtyard (5)
10. Songs for advertising (7)
11. Cane spirit (3)
13. Enlarging viewer (9)
14. Water boiler (6)
16. Abhor (6)
18. Having low intelligence (9)
20. Droop (3)
22. Wild duck (7)
23. Copy on thin paper (5)
25. Matters remaining (8)
26. Exclude (4)

## Down

1. Writing material (5)
2. Appropriate (3)
4. Coax (6)
5. Skill (7)
6. Observers (9)
7. Cut up (7)
8. Sea vessel (4)
12. Small spheres of camphor or naphthalene (9)
14. Indian state (7)
15. Dancer's one-piece costume (7)
17. Blurred mark (6)
19. Musical instrument (4)
21. Formal visitor (5)
24. Objective (3)

solution on page 209

# Puzzle 121

## Across

7. Continent (6)
8. Grave or gloomy in character (British, 6)
10. Gist (7)
11. Set or keep apart (5)
12. Cipher (4)
13. Uncanny, eerie (5)
17. Obvious and dull (5)
18. Bloc (4)
22. Held on tightly (5)
23. Cookery (7)
24. Pal (6)
25. Moves to music (6)

## Down

1. Resistance against attack (7)
2. Holy war (7)
3. Pay out (5)
4. Shaved crown of a monk's head (7)
5. Higher up (5)
6. Type of boat used to transport people and cars (5)
9. The relation of something to the matter at hand (9)
14. Line touching curve (7)
15. Defunct (7)
16. Charge falsely or with malicious intent (7)
19. Gibe, mock (5)
20. Loose fitting garment (5)
21. Roll of tobacco (5)

solution on page 210

# Puzzle 122

## Across

1. Former Nigerian capital (5)
4. Great gap (5)
10. Treat as a celebrity (7)
11. Not given food (5)
12. Boadicea's tribe (5)
13. Rapid rise (7)
15. Units of electrical resistance (4)
17. Great feast (5)
19. Perfume (5)
22. As far as (2,2)
25. Freakish (7)
27. Images in solid form (5)
29. Punctuation mark (5)
30. Collected (7)
31. Eastern (5)
32. Taut (5)

## Down

2. Superior (5)
3. Point of view (7)
5. Drags (5)
6. Food colorant (7)
7. British Prime Minister (5)
8. Muslim lady (5)
9. Snake (5)
14. Exclamation, hissing sound (4)
16. Period of time (4)
18. Complex proteins (7)
20. Money (7)
21. Sternwards (5)
23. Nut (5)
24. Away (5)
26. Lariat (5)
28. Desert well (5)

 solution on page 210

# Puzzle 123

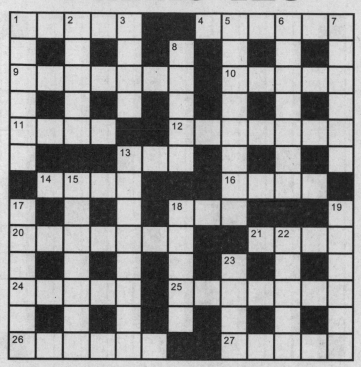

## Across

**1.** Scriptures (5)
**4.** Meat pin (6)
**9.** Small ships (7)
**10.** Fountain nymph (5)
**11.** Land force (4)
**12.** In quick tempo (7)
**13.** Zero (3)
**14.** Donate (4)
**16.** Christmas (4)
**18.** Embrace (3)
**20.** Skill (7)
**21.** Pace (4)
**24.** —— Dingo; Crocodile Dundee II actor (5)
**25.** Open gallery (7)
**26.** Struggle (6)
**27.** Difficulty (5)

## Down

**1.** Song (6)
**2.** Muslim lady of rank (5)
**3.** Dueling sword (4)
**5.** Tinder (8)
**6.** Squirm (7)
**7.** Furious (3-3)
**8.** Normal (5)
**13.** Film report (8)
**15.** Batting team (7)
**17.** Consequence (6)
**18.** Lift up with effort (5)
**19.** Scatter water (6)
**22.** Article of faith (5)
**23.** Curved structure (4)

**solution on page 210**

# Puzzle 124

## Across

1. Dwarf (5)
4. Drop-out (5)
10. Lottery game (7)
11. Belonging to the nose (5)
12. Prospect (5)
13. Flowers (7)
15. Unit of heredity (4)
17. Foreign (5)
19. Make up for (5)
22. Guessing game (1-3)
25. Gaelic dance evening (7)
27. Fake jewelry (5)
29. Dowdy woman (5)
30. Bishop's see (7)
31. Molars (5)
32. Grunt (5)

## Down

2. Designates (5)
3. Anchorage (7)
5. Old Greek dialect (5)
6. Ardor (7)
7. Musical staff (5)
8. Domestic cock (5)
9. Ecstasy (5)
14. Harvest crop (4)
16. —— Blyton, author (4)
18. Spare time (7)
20. Cyclone (7)
21. Jeer (5)
23. Partial darkness (5)
24. Disease (5)
26. Energy supplied (5)
28. Pointed weapon (5)

solution on page 211

# Puzzle 125

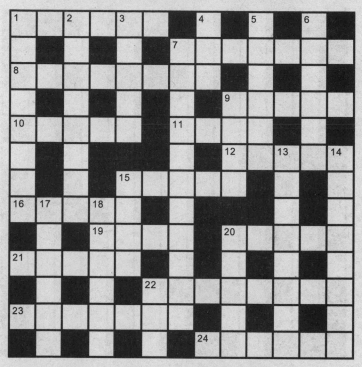

## Across

1. Artist's crayon (6)
7. Modernized (7)
8. Plentiful (8)
9. Brightest feature of Cygnus (5)
10. Avid (5)
11. Lord (4)
12. Very tired (3,2)
15. —— pole (5)
16. Passenger ship (5)
19. Pack of cards (4)
20. Move furtively (5)
21. Film star —— Murphy (5)
22. Hollow-horned ruminant (8)
23. Entering (7)
24. Growing area (6)

## Down

1. Quiet (8)
2. Large fish (8)
3. Senior (5)
4. Fitting (3)
5. Nurse Edith —— (6)
6. Middle Easterner (6)
7. Enterprise (11)
9. Tot of spirits (4)
13. Innkeeper (8)
14. Number (8)
15. Wood plant (4)
17. Halogen element (6)
18. Newsman (6)
20. Tuscan city (5)
22. Social insect (3)

solution on page 211

# Puzzle 126

## Across

4. Very weak (6)
5. Skin blemish (4)
7. Disagree (7)
10. Indian ruler (5)
11. Artificial human (7)
12. Fashion (5)
14. Cover (7)
15. Arabian spirit (5)
16. Blinded temporarily (7)
20. Person of fixed ideas (5)
21. Getting on (7)
22. Birthplace of mankind (4)
23. Referee (6)

## Down

1. —— Sanderson, British javelin thrower (5)
2. Secreting structure in animals (5)
3. Bullfighter (7)
4. Frustrate (4)
6. Drinking vessel (6)
8. Beg (7)
9. Circus swing (7)
10. Held firmly (7)
13. Compose (6)
14. Bereft of spouse (7)
17. Andean mammal (5)
18. Old Nick (5)
19. Sticky paste (4)

solution on page 211

# Puzzle 127

## Across

1. Substitute (6)
4. Flower leaf (5)
8. Vice (TV series) (5)
9. Storm around (7)
10. Sediment (7)
11. Flightless bird (4)
12. Recede (3)
14. Rear part (4)
15. Reverberate (4)
18. Fast-running Australian bird (3)
21. English painter (4)
23. Famous (7)
25. Cross-breed (7)
26. Freshwater creature (5)
27. Characteristic (5)
28. Thoroughfare (6)

## Down

1. Harm (6)
2. Playerless piano (7)
3. Three-sided figure (8)
4. Grandeur (4)
5. Garbage (5)
6. Elbow-room (6)
7. Written work (5)
13. Red vegetable (8)
16. Frequenter (7)
17. Recluse (6)
19. Male relative (5)
20. Small vicious animal (6)
22. Friendly Islands (5)
24. Gravel (4)

solution on page 212

# Puzzle 128

## Across

1. Decorative layer (6)
4. Procrastinate (5)
8. Fall out of date (5)
9. European country (7)
10. Learned (7)
11. Carved image (4)
12. Drinking vessel (3)
14. Engage as gears (4)
15. Peruvian Indian (4)
18. Digit (3)
21. Snare (4)
23. Photographing (1-6)
25. Tan (7)
26. Wooden wares (5)
27. Indian lute (5)
28. Sparse (6)

## Down

1. Silk fabric (6)
2. Sea-god (7)
3. Vision (8)
4. Rush (4)
5. Ghastly (5)
6. Per annum (6)
7. Women's quarters (5)
13. Enormous (8)
16. Famous war in the Ukraine (7)
17. Needle (6)
19. Bring to bear (5)
20. Means (6)
22. At a distance (5)
24. God of thunder (4)

solution on page 212

# Puzzle 129

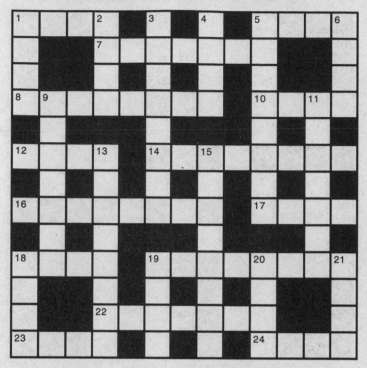

## Across

1. Aggressive rock music (4)
5. Whirring sound (4)
7. Women's game (7)
8. Inn (8)
10. Squirrel's nest (4)
12. Steering apparatus (4)
14. Trend (8)
16. Common hedge bush (8)
17. Substantive (4)
18. Heavenly body (4)
19. Liveliness (8)
22. Place of study (7)
23. Mark of lash (4)
24. Spirit (4)

## Down

1. Essence (4)
2. Nautical mile (4)
3. Narrow pointed shoe heel (8)
4. Endearingly crazy (4)
5. Stout club (8)
6. Gem (4)
9. Working (7)
11. Form a hard coating (7)
13. Motherly (8)
15. Number (8)
18. Slaughtered (4)
19. Small medicine bottle (4)
20. Minstrel songs (4)
21. Yell out, as with pain (4)

solution on page 212

# Puzzle 130

## Across

4. Ship's lounge (6)
5. Sign of the future (4)
7. Swerve (7)
10. Make up for (5)
11. Meat cake (7)
12. Harmonious sounds (5)
14. Ruler (7)
15. Distinctive smell (5)
16. Water jug (7)
20. Play for time (5)
21. Otitis (7)
22. Welsh resort (4)
23. Boyfriend to whom one intends to get married (6)

## Down

1. Stylistic talent (5)
2. Bards (5)
3. Non-professional (7)
4. Type of fat (4)
6. Papal legate (6)
8. Postal service for overseas (7)
9. Core, meaning (7)
10. Hospital social worker (7)
13. Speaker (6)
14. Hires (7)
17. Custom (5)
18. Wet (5)
19. Foot-covering (4)

solution on page 213

# Puzzle 131

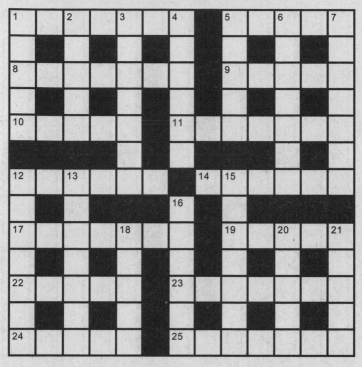

The answers in this crossword are anagrams of their clues, but can you discover the correct anagram in every case? (For instance, the solution to a clue such as 'Adder' could be either 'Dared' or 'Dread'... the choice isn't always obvious!)

## Across

**1.** A tum ass (7)
**5.** Me, sir! (5)
**8.** His pair (7)
**9.** Gnaws (5)
**10.** Drain (5)
**11.** On my ear (7)
**12.** Hew sec (6)
**14.** In duet (6)
**17.** Rate use (7)
**19.** A punt (5)
**22.** I bald (2-3)
**23.** Have ice (7)
**24.** Owned (5)
**25.** A red cay (7)

## Down

**1.** Satin (5)
**2.** Tried (5)
**3.** No usher (7)
**4.** Pea pal (6)
**5.** My tis (5)
**6.** To spear (7)
**7.** Wagered (7)
**12.** Manatee (7)
**13.** Sad Celt (7)
**15.** Gay hunt (7)
**16.** Lard he (6)
**18.** Below (5)
**20.** An ear (5)
**21.** He met (5)

# Puzzle 132

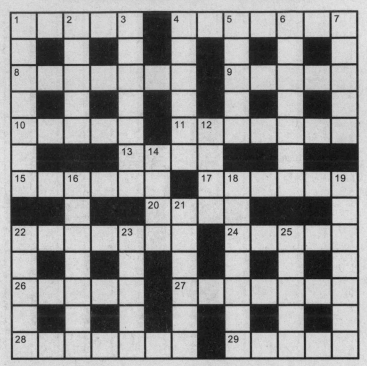

## Across

1. African tribesmen (5)
4. Examiner of accounts (7)
8. Portion (7)
9. Ecclesiastical vestments (5)
10. Front (5)
11. Smartened up (7)
13. Roster (4)
15. Greek 'I' (6)
17. Crimean commander (6)
20. Russian emperor (4)
22. Great joy (7)
24. Varieties (5)
26. Smithy (5)
27. Front tooth (7)
28. Let in again (7)
29. Enlist (5)

## Down

1. Full of relish (7)
2. Art of reasoning accurately (5)
3. Aircraft waiter (7)
4. Affirm by oath (6)
5. Furnishings (5)
6. In the news (7)
7. Demolished (5)
12. Airborne soldier (4)
14. Pledge (4)
16. Infectious disease (7)
18. Journalistic feature (7)
19. Breathing hole (7)
21. Exact (6)
22. Put off (5)
23. Glimmer (5)
25. Problem (5)

**solution on page 213**

# Puzzle 133

## Across

4. Sartorially smart (6)
5. Hoax (4)
7. Divide into four (7)
10. Fury (5)
11. Impressive display (7)
12. Brings up (5)
14. Plane terminal (7)
15. Game fish (5)
16. Deluge (7)
20. Civic leader (5)
21. Lockjaw (7)
22. Drag (4)
23. Prickly sensation (6)

## Down

1. Musical entertainment (5)
2. Measure (5)
3. Bright color (7)
4. Smear (4)
6. Ripe (6)
8. Betrayer of country (7)
9. Defensive mound (7)
10. Authorization (7)
13. Circlet of leaves (6)
14. Teleprompter (7)
17. Uncanny (5)
18. Dance (5)
19. Dandy (4)

solution on page 214

# Puzzle 134

## Across

1. Concert place (5)
4. Mother superior (6)
9. Impassioned, rhapsodic (7)
10. Tobacco product (5)
11. Type of fat (4)
12. Practicality (7)
13. Tear apart (3)
14. Flowering shrub (4)
16. Continuous discomfort (4)
18. Airplane (3)
20. Stoppage (7)
21. Long detailed story (4)
24. Musical ornament (5)
25. Graceful (7)
26. Medicinal plant (6)
27. Roofer (5)

## Down

1. Overnight case (6)
2. Cheek (5)
3. Engrave (4)
5. French card game (8)
6. Language (7)
7. Economize (6)
8. Drink noisily (5)
13. Not a monarchy (8)
15. Wearing away (7)
17. Nova —— (6)
18. Gem (5)
19. Trade by exchange (6)
22. Be of service (5)
23. Great achievement (4)

solution on page 214

# Puzzle 135

## Across

1. Medicinal pill (6)
4. Annoyed (5)
8. Titles (5)
9. Pain in lower back (7)
10. Puzzles (7)
11. Eyelid swelling (4)
12. Can (3)
14. Chime (4)
15. Slightly open (4)
18. Sheep (3)
21. Opulent (4)
23. Bodily indication (7)
25. Commend (7)
26. Semi-precious stone (5)
27. Bring to bear (5)
28. Solve crime (6)

## Down

1. Bicycle for two (6)
2. Italian child (7)
3. Outfit (8)
4. Charitable gifts (4)
5. Allowance (5)
6. Country gentlemen (6)
7. Explosion (5)
13. Sicken (8)
16. Flatter (7)
17. Mysterious (6)
19. Aigrette (5)
20. Conquer (6)
22. Clump of trees (5)
24. Protrude lips (4)

solution on page 214

# Puzzle 136

## Across

1. Opulence (6)
7. Transference (7)
8. Given back (8)
9. Crooked (5)
10. Plant exudation (5)
11. Old Mogul capital (4)
12. Catcall (5)
15. Clemency (5)
16. S African golfer Els (5)
19. Prefix meaning a million (4)
20. Percussion instruments (5)
21. Sprang (5)
22. Electrical connection (8)
23. Questioned (7)
24. Would-be catcher (6)

## Down

1. Clothes closet (8)
2. Political murderer (8)
3. Prickle (5)
4. Marry (3)
5. Tiny Japanese tree (6)
6. Belvedere (6)
7. Sent back to country of origin (11)
9. Fighting force (4)
13. Seasonal (8)
14. US painter (8)
15. Bump into (4)
17. Breed of monkey (6)
18. Reveal (6)
20. Little devil (5)
22. Quoits target (3)

solution on page 215

# Puzzle 137

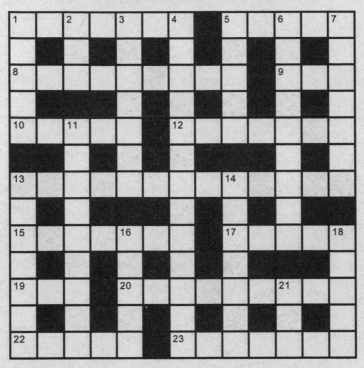

## Across

1. Bus depots, for example (7)
5. One who looks after a sick relative (5)
8. Set free (9)
9. Bounder (3)
10. Pedestrianized public square (5)
12. Nonsynthetic (7)
13. Cultivating (13)
15. Keep (7)
17. —— and lows (5)
19. Biblical man (3)
20. Everywhere (3,6)
22. Classroom fool (5)
23. Cricket throws (7)

## Down

1. Spring flowering plant (5)
2. Chest bone (3)
3. Encroachments (7)
4. On purpose (13)
5. Military trainee (5)
6. Repeating (9)
7. Warning signal (3,4)
11. Entry fee (9)
13. Go down (7)
14. Sticker (7)
16. Proverb (5)
18. Faces (5)
21. Employ (3)

# Puzzle 138

## Across

1. Monastery (5)
3. Item of food associated with Shrove Tuesday (7)
6. Make passing reference to (7)
8. City in West Yorkshire (5)
10. Short note sent between mobile phones (4,7)
12. Bellow (4)
13. Imitate (5)
15. Aromatic herb (4)
17. Thick soup of meat and vegetables (6,5)
19. Tag (5)
20. Imploring (7)
21. City in Washington (7)
22. Molten rock (5)

## Down

1. Protective suit, worn in combat (6)
2. This or that (6)
3. Play on words (3)
4. Board game (5)
5. Christian celebration (6)
7. Without reservation or exception (8)
9. Ancestry (8)
10. Ballroom dance (5)
11. Muslim name for God (5)
14. Book of the Bible (6)
15. Symbol of disgrace (6)
16. Something that baffles understanding (6)
18. Act of stealing (5)
20. Honey-producing insect (3)

solution on page 215

# Puzzle 139

The answers in this crossword are anagrams of their clues, but can you discover the correct anagram in every case? (For instance, the solution to a clue such as 'Adder' could be either 'Dared' or 'Dread'... the choice isn't always obvious!)

## Across

**2.** Dub (3)
**5.** In brace (7)
**8.** Late (4)
**9.** Leap (4)
**11.** Not (3)
**14.** A recoil (7)
**15.** Bored it (7)
**16.** Dad (3)
**18.** Abet (4)
**20.** Ekes (4)
**21.** Bare Leo (7)
**22.** Cat (3)

## Down

**1.** Bug loam (7)
**3.** Name (4)
**4.** Span (4)
**6.** Toy bean (7)
**7.** Near rim (7)
**10.** Nap (3)
**11.** Eat (3)
**12.** Don (3)
**13.** Ape (3)
**17.** Citadel (7)
**19.** Rate (4)
**20.** Boss (4)

# Puzzle 140

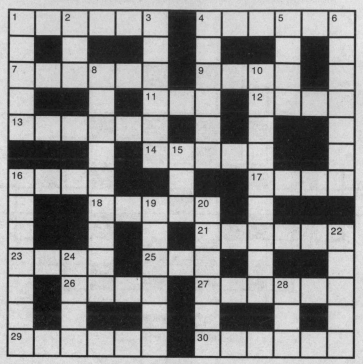

## Across

**1.** King who died at the Battle of Hastings (6)
**4.** Corkscrew (6)
**7.** Dissertation (6)
**9.** Concluding (4)
**11.** Epoch (3)
**12.** Toll (4)
**13.** Navy man (6)
**14.** Fastening (5)
**16.** Phonograph record (4)
**17.** Pay close attention to (4)
**18.** Bring upon oneself (5)
**21.** Total (6)
**23.** Threesome (4)
**25.** Lip (3)
**26.** Trickle (4)
**27.** Detestable (6)
**29.** Item used to brew a hot drink (6)
**30.** Utilize (6)

## Down

**1.** Despises (5)
**2.** Fish eggs (3)
**3.** Arid region (6)
**4.** Highly seasoned fatty sausage (6)
**5.** Speed of progress (4)
**6.** Region of northern Europe (7)
**8.** Lawyer (9)
**10.** Long strings of pasta (9)
**15.** Not me (3)
**16.** Tooth doctor (7)
**19.** Floor covering (6)
**20.** Distant (6)
**22.** Literary composition (5)
**24.** Thought (4)
**28.** Nocturnal bird of prey (3)

solution on page 216

# Puzzle 141

## Across

7. Gas found in air (6)
8. Amongst (6)
9. Not yet unsealed (8)
10. Nocturnal mammal (3)
11. Effete (8)
13. Extinct bird of Mauritius (4)
14. Tantalize (4)
16. Called with fluctuating voice (8)
18. Hen's produce (3)
19. More alien (8)
22. Respiratory disorder (6)
23. Hold back (6)

## Down

1. Alibi (6)
2. Unlearned (8)
3. Leg joint (4)
4. Gifted (8)
5. Cone-bearing tree (3)
6. Ground surrounded by water (6)
12. Native of Cairo, for example (8)
13. Conference attendee (8)
15. Month (6)
17. Common garden insect (6)
20. Measure of land (4)
21. For what reason? (3)

solution on page 216

# Puzzle 142

## Across

**1.** Swap goods (6)
**4.** Narrative song (6)
**8.** Gangway (5)
**10.** Fertile tract in desert (5)
**11.** Happen again (5)
**12.** Nursemaid (5)
**14.** Birds' homes (5)
**16.** Painting, sculpture, etc (3)
**18.** Bloc (4)
**19.** Curse (4)
**21.** Pigpen (3)
**24.** Broker (5)
**27.** Trust (5)
**29.** Cocktail fruit (5)
**30.** Pine (5)
**31.** Jeweled headdress (5)
**32.** Sewing tool (6)
**33.** Flail (6)

## Down

**1.** Clever (6)
**2.** Thick sap from tree (5)
**3.** Each (5)
**5.** Fruit of oak (5)
**6.** Endures (5)
**7.** Refrain, stop (6)
**9.** Mark left by wound (4)
**13.** Impeached US president (5)
**15.** Additional (5)
**16.** Beast of burden (3)
**17.** Plaything (3)
**20.** Deep ravine (6)
**22.** Part of animal (4)
**23.** Case for knife (6)
**25.** Wipe off (5)
**26.** Relating to variations in pitch (5)
**27.** Get (5)
**28.** Effigy (5)

solution on page 217

# Puzzle 143

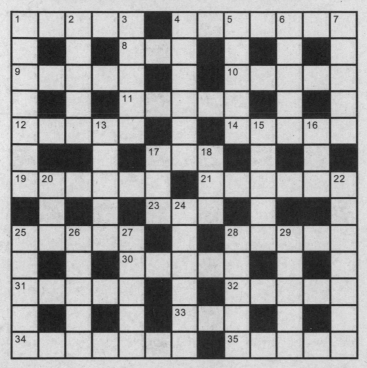

## Across

1. Noxious gases (5)
4. Cast aside (7)
8. Employ (3)
9. What 12 Across might do (5)
10. Month (5)
11. Kill by submerging in water (5)
12. Poetry (5)
14. Woman's marriage settlement (5)
17. Consumed (3)
19. Keep (6)
21. Fungal, mossy growth (6)
23. Remove moisture from (3)
25. Celestial body (5)
28. Fire-raising (5)
30. Accumulate (5)
31. Order of Greek architecture (5)
32. Varlet (5)
33. Be in debt (3)
34. Make level (7)
34. Breezy (5)

## Down

1. Eternally (7)
2. Town dignitary (5)
3. Leather with a napped surface (5)
4. Expel from a country (6)
5. Place upright (5)
6. Pointer (5)
7. Postpone (5)
13. Judder (5)
15. Happen (5)
16. Regret (3)
17. As well as (3)
18. Cambridgeshire city (3)
20. Inflated pride (3)
22. Convent (7)
24. Rationality (6)
25. Principal (5)
26. Irrational passion (5)
27. Implied (5)
28. Lopsided (5)
29. European kingdom (5)

solution on page 217

# Puzzle 144

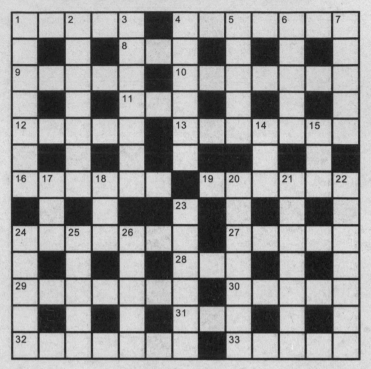

## Across

1. Engrave (5)
4. Thief (7)
8. Fuss (3)
9. At no time (5)
10. Feeblest (7)
11. Water barrier (3)
12. Smell (British, 5)
13. Female thespian (7)
16. Conundrum (6)
19. Offensive inquisitiveness (6)
24. Take for granted (7)
27. Digit, number (5)
28. Appropriate (3)
29. Whatever happens to be available (3,4)
30. Long raised strip (5)
31. Flightless bird (3)
32. More clearly defined (7)
33. Wall painting (5)

## Down

1. Make allowances for (7)
2. Square cases of dough with savory fillings (7)
3. Tympanic membrane (7)
4. Archer (6)
5. Show a response (5)
6. Vassal (5)
7. Religious rituals (5)
14. Shaft of light (3)
15. Male child (3)
17. Neither (3)
18. Oxygen, for instance (3)
20. Pulpit (7)
21. Encroacher (7)
22. Civilized, cultured (7)
23. Drinking cup (6)
24. Tubes (5)
25. Additional (5)
26. Take control of (5)

solution on page 217

# Puzzle 145

## Across

1. Defect (5)
4. Small fish (7)
8. Big (5)
9. Firmness of purpose (7)
10. Contrary (7)
11. Freshwater fish (5)
12. Join the military (6)
14. Hood (6)
18. Not affected by alcohol (5)
20. Flower (7)
22. Deviation from the common rule (7)
23. Body (5)
24. Intrigued (7)
25. Triangular area where a river divides (5)

## Down

1. Leaves (7)
2. Disentangle (7)
3. Belonging to them (5)
4. Surface on which pictures can be projected (6)
5. Italian rice dish (7)
6. Eskimo's home (5)
7. Throw out (5)
13. Caustic remark (7)
15. Part of the nose (7)
16. Lottery (7)
17. Conformed (6)
18. Remains (5)
19. Thin, meat soup (5)
21. Decided (5)

solution on page 218

# Puzzle 146

## Across

1. Feline animal (3)
3. Ordered series (5)
8. Magic lantern man (5)
9. Pudding accompaniment (7)
10. Museum custodian (7)
11. V-shaped indentation (5)
12. Royal residence (6)
14. Blazing (6)
18. Board game (5)
20. Italian dish (7)
22. Protect from impact (7)
23. Bring up (5)
24. Great (5)
25. Droop (3)

## Down

1. In the middle (7)
2. Stealing (5)
3. Safe (6)
4. Arms stash (7)
5. Precise (5)
6. Breadth (5)
7. Breakfast food container (6)
13. Bank clerk (7)
15. Getting bigger (7)
16. Saucepan stand (6)
17. He might live in 12 Across (6)
18. Hot chocolate (5)
19. Artist's tripod (5)
21. Micro-organism (5)

solution on page 218

# Puzzle 147

## Across

1. Foodstore (6)
4. Counting implement (6)
8. Northern English city (5)
10. Loud (5)
11. Item (5)
12. Not easy to swallow (5)
14. Corpulent (5)
16. Snake (3)
18. Owl's cry (4)
19. First man (4)
21. Young newt (3)
24. Despised (5)
27. Hi (5)
29. Lessen (5)
30. Spiritual leader (5)
31. Proportion (5)
32. Wanders (6)
33. Vigor (6)

## Down

1. Lawkeeping force (6)
2. Female relative (5)
3. Out of practice (5)
5. Lotto (5)
6. Noise of bell (5)
7. Fashions (6)
9. Prejudice (4)
13. Entire (5)
15. Couple (5)
16. Took a meal (3)
17. Tap lightly (3)
20. Choir (6)
22. Level (4)
23. Settlement (6)
25. Fleshy root (5)
26. Lawn flower (5)
27. Wading bird (5)
28. At a point further ahead in time (5)

solution on page 218

# Puzzle 148

## Across

1. Knot with two loops and loose ends (3)
3. Form (5)
8. Memory loss (7)
9. Post at the top or bottom of a flight of stairs (5)
10. Yellow-orange to orange color (5)
11. Feel (7)
12. Speeding (6)
14. Spine-bearing, succulent plant (6)
18. Cutting up (7)
20. Somber (5)
22. Hang back (5)
23. In an open manner (7)
24. Empower (5)
25. Male offspring (3)

## Down

1. Long seat for more than one person (5)
2. Occidental (7)
3. Pure (6)
4. Extension to main building (5)
5. Fine particles of wood (7)
6. Divide by two (5)
7. Prefer (British, 6)
13. The dead body of an animal (7)
15. Localized ulcer or sore (7)
16. Wanders (6)
17. Take no notice of (6)
18. Captivate (5)
19. Lazed (5)
21. Object used by a conductor to direct an orchestra (5)

solution on page 219

# Puzzle 149

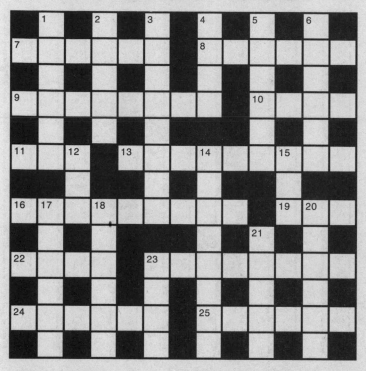

## Across

7. Cream-filled pastry (6)
8. Of value (6)
9. Willing to give (8)
10. Extremely wicked (4)
11. Beast of burden (3)
13. Sweetheart (9)
16. Tall pole on which ensign is raised (9)
19. Wane (3)
22. Addition (4)
23. Climbing, flowering shrub (8)
24. Decapitate (6)
25. Purple flower (6)

## Down

1. Get at (6)
2. Humped beast (5)
3. Self-important (8)
4. Rock salmon (4)
5. Choose (6)
6. Painful swelling of the big toe (6)
12. Ocean (3)
14. Gushing (8)
15. Wrath (3)
17. Made calm or still (6)
18. Ring for sealing a pipe joint (6)
20. Water heater (6)
21. At a lower place (5)
23. Walk through water (4)

# Puzzle 150

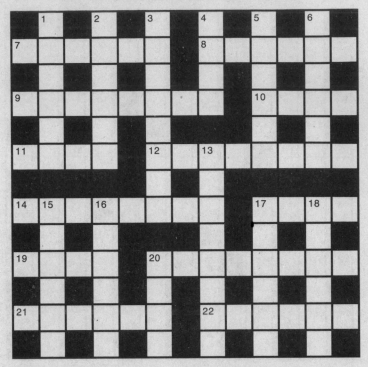

## Across

7. North American nation (6)
8. Mass departure (6)
9. Knitted jacket (8)
10. Daddy (4)
11. Fluid-filled sac (4)
12. Firm in purpose or belief (8)
14. Slaughterhouse (8)
17. Naked (4)
19. Arrived (4)
20. Trounce (8)
21. It's XI in Roman numerals (6)
22. Shifty deceptive person (6)

## Down

1. Yellow songbird (6)
2. Brigand (6)
3. Pouched mammal (8)
4. Introduce to solid food (4)
5. New Testament book telling the story of Christ (6)
6. End product (6)
13. Sing and play for somebody (8)
15. Former minor parish official (6)
16. One dozen (6)
17. Confines (6)
18. Reposed (6)
20. Wind direction pointer (4)

solution on page 219

# Puzzle 151

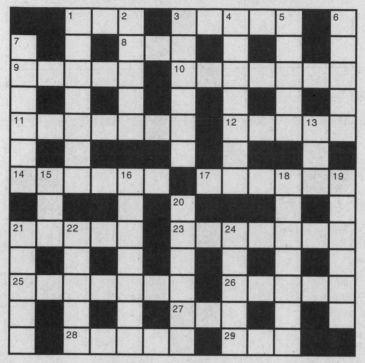

## Across

1. Cacophony (3)
3. Fundamental (5)
8. Alcoholic brew (3)
9. Greek tale teller (5)
10. Seedless raisin (7)
11. Laid out (7)
12. Nick (5)
14. Acid in vinegar (6)
17. Superior (6)
21. Token that postal fees have been paid (5)
23. Gives expression to (7)
25. Native of Tel Aviv, for example (7)
26. Afflicted by illness (5)
27. Appropriate (3)
28. Artist's tripod (5)
29. Conclude (3)

## Down

1. Merit (7)
2. Diaper (5)
3. Next to (6)
4. Hush (7)
5. Repetitive song (5)
6. Shore (5)
7. Crescent-shaped yellow fruit (6)
13. Rod used to play snooker (3)
15. Crib (3)
16. Have an emotional or cognitive impact upon (7)
18. Set about dealing with (7)
19. Dwell (6)
20. Abnegation (6)
21. Canonized person (5)
22. Concur (5)
24. Feeling extreme anger (5)

solution on page 220

# Puzzle 152

## Across

1. Dingy (6)
4. Fit out (6)
8. Volley (5)
10. Wealthy man (5)
11. One of three equal parts (5)
12. Repletes (5)
14. Torment (5)
16. Painting, sculpture, etc (3)
18. Painful sore (4)
19. Bitter (4)
21. Recede (3)
24. Norse goddess (5)
27. Serenity (5)
29. Receive (5)
30. Picture puzzle (5)
31. Concur (5)
32. Gaped (6)
33. Spit (6)

## Down

1. Refrain (6)
2. Acclaim (5)
3. Sources (5)
5. Girl's name (5)
6. Forbidden (5)
7. Fertilized egg (6)
9. Coffin support (4)
13. Coal black (5)
15. Filth (5)
16. Alcoholic brew (3)
17. Bill in a restaurant (3)
20. Fracas (6)
22. Support (4)
23. Shooting star (6)
25. Arm joint (5)
26. Gangway (5)
27. Trick (5)
28. Projectile shot from a bow (5)

solution on page 220

# Puzzle 153

## Across

1. Brilliant (6)
4. Type of tree (6)
8. Stonecutter (5)
10. Relative by marriage (2-3)
11. Severe and unremitting (5)
12. With the mouth wide open as in wonder or awe (5)
14. Torment (5)
16. Wrath (3)
18. Wound, harm (4)
19. At another time (4)
21. Equality (3)
24. Goodbye (5)
27. Attaching (5)
29. Strong, lightweight wood (5)
30. System of principles or beliefs (5)
31. Telegraph (5)
32. Genteel (6)
33. Strain (6)

## Down

1. Primate (6)
2. Civil or military authority in Turkey (5)
3. Use water to remove soap (5)
5. Crockery (5)
6. Stringed instrument (5)
7. Ever (6)
9. Antlered animal (4)
13. Woodworking tool (5)
15. State of high honor (5)
16. Pixie (3)
17. Sense organ (3)
20. Daredevil (6)
22. Wheel shaft (4)
23. The act of coming out (6)
25. Perfect (5)
26. Submersible warship, associated with WWII (1-4)
27. Implied (5)
28. Permeate (5)

solution on page 220

# Puzzle 154

## Across

**1.** Exhibition of cowboy skills (5)
**4.** Device used to hold a carpet in place (7)
**7.** French river (5)
**8.** Rushed (5)
**10.** Rod used to play snooker (3)
**11.** Flightless bird (3)
**12.** Apprehension (5)
**14.** Town dignitary (5)
**15.** Campanologist (6)
**18.** Esteems (6)
**22.** Scrub (5)
**23.** Piece of poetry (5)
**26.** Popular drink (3)
**27.** Large monkey (3)
**28.** Bracing, brisk (5)
**30.** Titan (5)
**31.** It's said to make the heart grow fonder (7)
**32.** Mettle (5)

## Down

**1.** Feeling of deep and bitter anger and ill-will (British, 7)
**2.** Drugged (5)
**3.** Oily fruit (5)
**4.** Avaricious (6)
**5.** Green vegetable (3)
**6.** Detector used to locate distant objects (5)
**8.** Cuban dance (5)
**9.** S American beaver-like rodent (5)
**13.** Piece of scrap material (5)
**16.** Snare (5)
**17.** Third planet from the sun (5)
**19.** Beat hard (3)
**20.** Any domain of knowledge acquired by systematic study (7)
**21.** Capital of the Czech republic (6)
**22.** Bulgarian capital (5)
**24.** Languish (5)
**25.** Consumer (5)
**29.** View (3)

solution on page 221

# Puzzle 155

## Across

1. Furrow (6)
4. Long-bodied reptile (6)
8. In the middle of (5)
10. Oneness (5)
11. Doorkeeper (5)
12. Lofty nest of a bird of prey (5)
14. Result (5)
16. Fountain (3)
18. Supplication (4)
19. Every one (4)
21. Fluffy scarf of feathers (3)
24. Right-hand page (5)
27. Marsh plant (5)
29. Act of stealing (5)
30. Continental quilt (5)
31. Eskimo's home (5)
32. Bodyguard (6)
33. The act of coming out (6)

## Down

1. Rock fragments and pebbles (6)
2. Smell (British, 5)
3. Undefined (5)
5. Harden (5)
6. Haywire (5)
7. John ——, English poet, 1631–1700 (6)
9. Item of footwear (4)
13. Cove (5)
15. A space set back or indented (5)
16. Prod (3)
17. Popular drink (3)
20. Grievance (6)
22. Concluded (4)
23. Courageous men (6)
25. Belonging to a city (5)
26. Freshwater carnivorous mammal (5)
27. Painful wound caused by a wasp (5)
28. Dig deeply into (5)

solution on page 221

# Puzzle 156

## Across

1. US state in the Rocky Mountains (5)
3. Sanction (7)
6. Dissent (7)
8. Tiny morsel of bread or cake (5)
10. System of words used in a particular discipline (11)
12. Highway (4)
13. Narrow backstreet (5)
15. Recount (4)
17. Feeling of evil to come (11)
19. Hard, dark wood (5)
20. Assumed, took as one's own child (7)
21. Lived (7)
22. Discourage (5)

## Down

1. Mar (6)
2. Repugnance (6)
3. Pretend (3)
4. Relating to the countryside (5)
5. Fertilized egg (6)
7. Milk pudding ingredient (8)
9. Inoculated with a hypodermic needle (8)
10. Item of furniture (5)
11. Many times (5)
14. Orb (6)
15. Tumble, collapse (6)
16. Food store (6)
18. Subtraction (5)
20. Sum up (3)

solution on page 221

# Puzzle 157

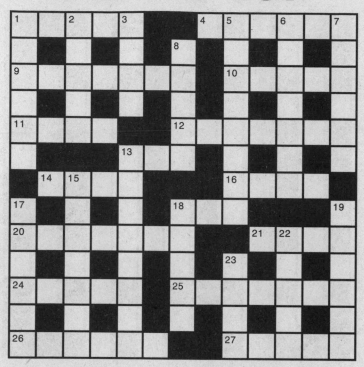

## Across

1. Slow learner (5)
4. Revised (6)
9. Imaginary animal (7)
10. All animal life of a place (5)
11. Told untruths (4)
12. Surgeon's knife (7)
13. Fire's remains (3)
14. Box (4)
16. Daintily pretty (4)
18. Chopper (3)
20. Full house (7)
21. Skin (4)
24. More (5)
25. Flight company (7)
26. Abundance (6)
27. Anthem (5)

## Down

1. Multiply by 2 (6)
2. Lacking sophistication (5)
3. Greek god of love (4)
5. Resistance (8)
6. Wind instrument (7)
7. Lethal (6)
8. Grind the teeth (5)
13. Haughty (8)
15. Painter's board (7)
17. Slumbering (6)
18. Map-collection (5)
19. Even if (6)
22. Live (5)
23. Streetcar (4)

solution on page 222

# Puzzle 158

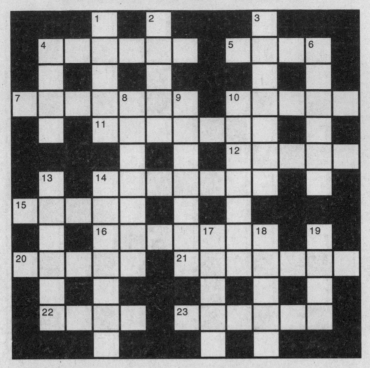

## Across

4. Unwell (6)
5. Expression (4)
7. Upgrade (7)
10. Hungarian composer (5)
11. Shoulder-ornament (7)
12. Triangular part of wall (5)
14. Prohibited (7)
15. North European river (5)
16. Unbeliever (7)
20. Famous explorer (5)
21. Least difficult (7)
22. Exchange (4)
23. Yarn (6)

## Down

1. Blaze (5)
2. Girl's name (5)
3. Performance (7)
4. Askew (4)
6. Gag (6)
8. Prosperous (7)
9. British Princess's name (7)
10. Envoys (7)
13. Strikes (6)
14. Beginning (7)
17. Russian country house (5)
18. Animate (5)
19. Second-hand (4)

solution on page 222

# Puzzle 159

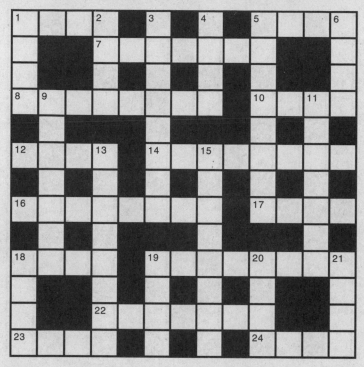

## Across

1. Organ of flight (4)
5. Stiff paper (4)
7. Accuse of treason (7)
8. Wide view (8)
10. Fluctuate (4)
12. Baby's bed (4)
14. Exciting novel or film (8)
16. Land-living amphibian (4,4)
17. Period of time (4)
18. Large scale (4)
19. Unnaturally high voice (8)
22. Rubbery (7)
23. Three feet (4)
24. Wolf-like scream (4)

## Down

1. Stinging insect (4)
2. Banking system (4)
3. Splash (8)
4. Facts given (4)
5. Quality of a knight (8)
6. Squirrel's nest (4)
9. Delivery from a plane or helicopter (3-4)
11. Play it again (2-5)
13. Transgressed, violated (8)
15. Adjust (8)
18. Grudging feeling (4)
19. Open tart (4)
20. Individually (4)
21. Gemstone (4)

solution on page 222

# Puzzle 160

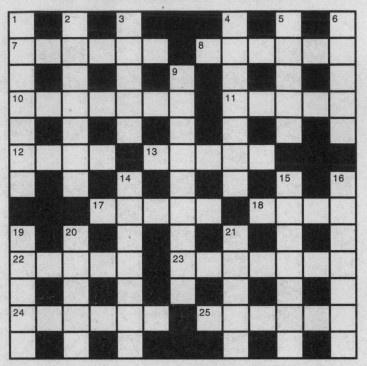

## Across

7. To descend by rope (6)
8. Generator (6)
10. Amused (7)
11. Month (5)
12. Major (4)
13. Operatic airs (5)
17. Roofing material (5)
18. S American Indian (4)
22. Fully mature (5)
23. Forestall (7)
24. Underground passage (6)
25. Wrongdoer (6)

## Down

1. Music of the 30s (7)
2. Mind reader (7)
3. Firearm (5)
4. Night attire (British, 7)
5. Wed (5)
6. Australian bear (5)
9. Worship (9)
14. Goods lost at sea (7)
15. Supernatural (7)
16. Fortified white wine (7)
19. Clerical house (5)
20. Tall fur hat (5)
21. Take advantage (5)

solution on page 223

# Puzzle 161

## Across

1. Relating to the written word (8)
5. Measure of land (4)
8. Male voice (8)
9. Poems (4)
11. Traders who retail novels, reference works, etc (11)
14. Fall behind (3)
16. Cowboy contest (5)
17. Pedal digit (3)
18. With long, slim lower limbs (7-4)
21. Orderly (4)
22. A veteran soldier (8)
24. Battle between two (4)
25. Woodwind instrument (8)

## Down

1. Part of the ear (4)
2. Pulse (5)
3. Going backwards (10)
4. Hasten (3)
6. Part of broken set (7)
7. Catastrophe (8)
10. Completely (10)
12. Grasslike marsh plant (5)
13. Confined in a small room (8)
15. Hot plate (7)
19. Enchantress (5)
20. Jape (4)
23. Pointed tool (3)

# Puzzle 162

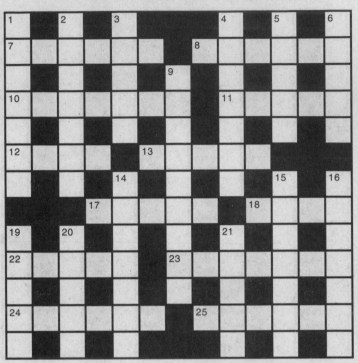

## Across

7. Hip (6)
8. Total uproar (6)
10. Draw back (7)
11. Nervous (5)
12. Elliptical (4)
13. 14 pounds (5)
17. Serious play (5)
18. Disfigurement (4)
22. Passage through church (5)
23. Harmful (7)
24. Unwholesome (6)
25. Sorcerer (6)

## Down

1. Old horse-drawn vehicle (7)
2. Of marriage (7)
3. Stony hillside (5)
4. Fate (7)
5. Solitary (5)
6. Dark brown (5)
9. Utterance (9)
14. Poison (7)
15. Learned person (7)
16. Holy war (7)
19. Mild and pleasant weather (5)
20. Appropriate (5)
21. Woodland plant (5)

solution on page 223

# Puzzle 163

## Across

1. Poe's house (5)
4. Musical staff (5)
10. Small mat (7)
11. Flavor (5)
12. Radioactive gas (5)
13. Bloodsucker (7)
15. Chilly (4)
17. Underworld god (5)
19. Message (5)
22. Ancient biblical city (4)
25. Pacify (7)
27. Egyptian capital (5)
29. Large antelope (5)
30. Scott novel (7)
31. Decorate (5)
32. Wading bird (5)

## Down

2. Burn (5)
3. Defunct (7)
5. Carved pole (5)
6. Trace (7)
7. Contempt (5)
8. Well done! (5)
9. Cross (5)
14. High male voice (4)
16. Seep (4)
18. Sheltered side (7)
20. Charm (7)
21. Land surrounded by water (5)
23. Asian country (5)
24. Senior member of group (5)
26. Royal family (5)
28. Watery humor (5)

solution on page 224

# Puzzle 164

## Across

7. Bird house (6)
8. Rain channel (6)
10. Open framework (7)
11. S American fox (5)
12. Oxfordshire (4)
13. Blood pump (5)
17. Thread (British, 5)
18. Travel permit (4)
22. Legend (5)
23. Ill-fated liner (7)
24. Landing-strip (6)
25. Misused (6)

## Down

1. Inflatable bag (7)
2. Invented narrative (7)
3. Educate (5)
4. Bird of prey (7)
5. Rear of ship (5)
6. Cavalry unit (5)
9. Make merry (9)
14. Ore (7)
15. Self-possession (7)
16. Waterfall (7)
19. Burning (5)
20. Cut of beef (1-4)
21. Cornstalks (5)

solution on page 224

# Solutions

## Puzzle 1

ACROSS:
1. Rip
3. Hesitate
7. Ogre
8. Warble
10. Himself
13. Egg
14. Row
16. Bastion
18. Viaduct
19. Eel
21. Owe
22. Escapee
25. Flaunt
27. Aver
28. Endanger
29. Key

DOWN:
1. Rather
2. Poem
3. Heal
4. Sow
5. Ambience
6. Emerge
9. Artistic
11. Emblazon
12. Fissure
15. Waveband
17. Coffee
20. Leeway
23. Star
24. Pork
26. Tag

## Puzzle 2

ACROSS:
1. Awash
4. Asinine
8. Elm
9. Space
10. Ozone
11. Liken
14. Ogle
16. Cyst
18. Gestapo
19. Deer
21. Bump
23. Elector
24. Cult
26. Apse
28. Stuck
31. Alive
32. Ensue
33. Owl
34. Pigskin
35. Plaid

DOWN:
1. Abscond
2. Avail
3. Heel
4. Amok
5. Icon
6. Ivory
7. Erect
12. Inspect
13. Elastic
15. Egret
16. Cobra
17. Sum
20. Emu
22. Pretend
24. Cramp
25. Lying
27. Pasta
28. Seek
29. Upon
30. Kelp

## Puzzle 3

ACROSS:
1. Sinful
4. Taurus
7. Nugget
9. Race
11. Hen
12. Lame
13. Azalea
14. Lapse
16. Saga
17. Need
18. Night
21. Agenda
23. Vows
25. Par
26. Eels
27. Grease
29. Esteem
30. Talent

DOWN:
1. Santa
2. Nag
3. Lethal
4. Turnip
5. Rhea
6. Severed
8. Galvanise
10. Clientele
15. Ash
16. Salvage
19. Gypsum
20. Target
22. Adept
24. Wept
28. Axe

## Puzzle 4

ACROSS:
1. House
3. New moon
6. Reunion
8. Adieu
10. Wisdom teeth
12. Wart
13. Slyly
15. Item
17. Agglomerate
19. Inure
20. Adrenal
21. Gumdrop
22. Often

DOWN:
1. Harrow
2. Sunlit
3. Nun
4. Midge
5. Nought
7. Old flame
9. Implored
10. Wrong
11. Elite
14. Paving
15. Itself
16. Muslin
18. Lurid
20. Asp

## Puzzle 5

ACROSS:
1. Stuck
3. Monsoon
6. Undergo
8. Snoop
10. Minimum wage
12. Knot
13. Given
15. Atop
17. Controversy
19. Equal
20. Womanly
21. Swollen
22. Elder

DOWN:
1. Squawk
2. Credit
3. Moo
4. Sinew
5. Nephew
7. Gridiron
9. Super-ego
10. Mourn
11. Amity
14. Access
15. Assail
16. Prayer
18. Trail
20. Wan

## Puzzle 6

ACROSS:
1. Slush
3. Leading
6. Upgrade
8. Acute
10. Clear-headed
12. Doll
13. Shiny
15. Raid
17. Stereotyped
19. Bible
20. Jubilee
21. Ratchet
22. Merit

DOWN:
1. Stupid
2. Scroll
3. Lie
4. Dacha
5. Greedy
7. Death row
9. Thank you
10. Close
11. Dread
14. Isobar
15. Refine
16. Deceit
18. Relic
20. Jot

## Puzzle 7

ACROSS:
1. Afford
4. Ocular
8. Adieu
9. Canape
10. Naked
12. Carousel
13. Sue
14. Won
15. Split-pea
18. Ennui
19. Unison
20. Angle
21. Winter
22. Amulet

DOWN:
1. Aback
2. Furnace
3. Dude
5. Counterpane
6. Links
7. Rundown
8. Appropriate
11. Quail
13. Somehow
14. Wassail
16. Onion
17. Unlit
19. Ulna

## Puzzle 8

ACROSS:
4. Tanned
5. Stye
7. Abolish
10. Depth
11. Enteric
12. Sheet
14. Re-enact
15. Baton
16. Estuary
20. Glade
21. Sidecar
22. Near
23. Slushy

DOWN:
1. Ankle
2. Feast
3. Utrecht
4. Tube
6. Either
8. Incense
9. Heinous
10. Discard
13. Raglan
14. Roedean
17. Aisle
18. Yeast
19. Baby

## Puzzle 9

ACROSS:
1. Laird
4. Ice-cap
9. Ballast
10. Tripe
11. Undo
12. Dickens
13. Doe
14. Knew
16. Mint
18. Orb
20. Buckled
21. Sofa
24. Tutti
25. Ulysses
26. Dredge
27. Extra

DOWN:
1. Labour
2. Idled
3. Dear
5. Catacomb
6. Crimean
7. Please
8. Etude
13. Dwelling
15. Necktie
17. Abated
18. Odium
19. Nausea
22. Onset
23. Byre

## Puzzle 10

ACROSS:
1. Pagan
4. Richard
8. Damping
9. Realm
10. Outdo
11. Rhubarb
13. Bade
15. Kaolin
17. Aghast
20. Tide
22. Digress
24. Nasal
26. Liner
27. Airlift
28. Alcohol
29. Candy

DOWN:
1. Padlock
2. Gamut
3. Nairobi
4. Regard
5. Corfu
6. Alabama
7. Demob
12. Head
14. Ants
16. Organic
18. Generic
19. Tolstoy
21. Israel
22. Delta
23. Earth
25. Scion

## Puzzle 11

ACROSS:
1. Biscuit
5. Comma
8. Scald
9. Rancour
10. Contradiction
11. Pirate
12. Coarse
15. Infinitesimal
18. Seabird
19. Egret
20. Sprig
21. Obscene

DOWN:
1. Basic
2. Scanner
3. Understand-ing
4. Tirade
5. Conscious-ness
6. Maori
7. Arrange
11. Priests
13. Remorse
14. Studio
16. Flair
17. Litre

## Puzzle 12

ACROSS:
7. Sliver
8. Chaste
10. Harlech
11. Roach
12. Loot
13. Elbow
17. Baulk
18. Lair
22. Brawl
23. Italian
24. Author
25. Slouch

DOWN:
1. Asphalt
2. Pierrot
3. Vexed
4. Cheroot
5. Oscar
6. Delhi
9. Chilblain
14. Balloon
15. Fatigue
16. Tranche
19. U-boat
20. Baste
21. Maple

## Puzzle 13

**ACROSS:**
1. Waltz
4. Harass
9. Divorce
10. Tease
11. Lurk
12. Mineral
13. Key
14. Flue
16. Memo
18. Sty
20. Hemlock
21. Weld
24. Orate
25. Terrace
26. Eroded
27. Exert

**DOWN:**
1. Waddle
2. Lover
3. Zero
5. Autonomy
6. Anagram
7. Steals
8. Jemmy
13. Kerosene
15. Lumbago
17. Chrome
18. Skate
19. Advent
22. Elate
23. Urge

## Puzzle 14

**ACROSS:**
1. Twig
5. Plug
7. Lyrical
8. Teenager
10. Tutu
12. Aged
14. Escapade
16. Agnostic
17. Swop
18. Odes
19. Optimist
22. Elegist
23. Snip
24. Hock

**DOWN:**
1. Tart
2. Glen
3. Fragment
4. Scar
5. Platypus
6. Guru
9. Engaged
11. Tedious
13. Doorstep
15. Cocktail
18. Opus
19. Oven
20. Moth
21. Task

## Puzzle 15

**ACROSS:**
1. Blot
3. Lopsided
9. Gorse
10. Trident
11. Lap
13. Traumatic
14. Client
16. Crisis
18. Waistcoat
20. Sue
22. Ruinous
23. Lapse
25. Speckled
26. Ploy

**DOWN:**
1. Bagel
2. Oar
4. Outlaw
5. Swimmer
6. Duettists
7. Detects
8. Vent
12. Primitive
14. Cowards
15. Network
17. Mousse
19. Toll
21. Enemy
24. Pal

## Puzzle 16

**ACROSS:**
1. Spade
3. Tabloid
6. Palette
8. Steal
10. Omnipresent
12. Next
13. Spays
15. Skim
17. Appropriate
19. Slide
20. Chatter
21. Rebound
22. Ocean

**DOWN:**
1. Siphon
2. Dreamt
3. Tee
4. Lotus
5. Dilate
7. Tailpipe
9. Crayfish
10. Oxlip
11. Evoke
14. Caesar
15. Static
16. Matron
18. Rodeo
20. Cud

## Puzzle 17

**ACROSS:**
1. Barren
4. Redeem
8. Nest
10. Cucumber
12. Elegance
13. Sofa
14. Mar
15. Tyranny
17. Orb
19. Atom
21. Overhear
22. Redolent
24. Ally
26. Parade
27. Rhesus

**DOWN:**
1. Bun
2. Retreat
3. Nuclear free
5. Emu
6. Emblem
7. Marjoram
9. Euro
11. Chain letter
13. Snowdrop
16. Yardage
18. Border
20. Oval
23. Lid
25. Yes

## Puzzle 18

**ACROSS:**
1. Sum
3. Strumpet
7. Ogre
8. Writer
10. Classic
13. Oar
15. Blindfold
17. Impromptu
19. Sip
21. Extrude
23. Locale
25. Agog
26. Chop suey
27. Ear

**DOWN:**
1. Stucco
2. Mohair
3. Semi
4. Raw
5. Potato
6. Torpid
9. Readjust
11. Subtotal
12. Cripple
14. Aim
16. Lei
17. Italic
18. Poncho
19. Smudge
20. Prefer
22. X-ray
24. Ecu

## Puzzle 19

ACROSS:
1. Becalm
4. Voiced
8. Glut
10. Wisteria
12. Immature
14. Noel
15. Son
16. Languid
18. Goa
20. Rigs
22. Roommate
23. Informer
26. Saga
28. Eulogy
29. Normal

DOWN:
1. Big
2. Anthill
3. Mow
5. Opt
6. Carves
7. Dead ends
9. Lido
11. Satsuma
13. Minimum
14. Negative
17. Dresser
19. Artful
21. Gang
24. Rug
25. Run
27. Awl

## Puzzle 20

ACROSS:
1. Hoard
4. Epaulet
8. Ill
9. Noble
10. Auger
11. Tenor
14. Bomb
16. Glib
18. Outplay
19. Glow
21. Peep
23. Erasers
24. Tail
26. Yore
28. Style
31. Idiot
32. Dream
33. Lag
34. Gumdrop
35. Yeast

DOWN:
1. Handbag
2. Album
3. Diet
4. Elan
5. Afar
6. Legal
7. Throb
12. Entrant
13. Oil well
15. Bowel
16. Gypsy
17. Ice
20. Lea
22. Pre-empt
24. Tying
25. Idiom
27. Opera
28. Stir
29. Yelp
30. Edgy

## Puzzle 21

ACROSS:
1. Piton
5. Block
8. Usage
9. Least
10. Inure
11. Thing
12. Apply
15. Emend
18. Boo
20. Bureau
21. Letter
22. Mad
24. Opine
27. Feast
30. Ruler
31. Drier
32. Owlet
33. Overt
34. Rotor
35. Haste

DOWN:
1. Polka
2. Tramp
3. Nutty
4. Calico
5. Beige
6. Ovule
7. Knead
13. Plump
14. Lie-in
16. Metre
17. Needs
18. Bum
19. Old
23. Asleep
24. Order
25. Idiot
26. Error
27. Froth
28. Atlas
29. Tithe

## Puzzle 22

ACROSS:
1. Attic
5. Incur
8. Round
9. Imbue
10. E-mail
11. Pizza
12. Usage
15. Lofty
18. Sew
20. Tundra
21. Escape
22. Cad
24. Calyx
27. Craze
30. Earth
31. Dozen
32. Input
33. Oriel
34. Resin
35. Lanky

DOWN:
1. Adieu
2. Tibia
3. Crepe
4. Guzzle
5. Ideal
6. Chaff
7. Rally
13. Scuba
14. Godly
16. Oscar
17. Topaz
18. Sac
19. Wed
23. Afraid
24. Cedar
25. Lazes
26. Xenon
27. Chill
28. Aspen
29. Entry

## Puzzle 23

ACROSS:
1. Among
4. Garland
8. Eel
9. Ruler
10. Uranium
11. Met
13. Inky
15. Bier
17. Ormolu
18. King
21. Dial
24. Upkeep
25. Okay
27. Town
29. For
31. Keynote
32. Image
33. Elf
34. Muskrat
35. Erect

DOWN:
1. Airsick
2. Oilskin
3. Germ
4. Glut
5. Roan
6. Alibi
7. Demur
12. Eureka
14. Bolero
15. Bud
16. Era
19. Ilk
20. Guy
22. Isolate
23. Lenient
25. Oakum
26. Abyss
28. Door
29. Feet
30. Rife

## Puzzle 24

ACROSS:
1. Hand
3. Parallel
9. Nasty
10. T-shirts
12. Epic
14. Cob
15. Eye
16. Old world
19. Foxy
20. Gone
22. Respired
23. Ate
25. Duo
27. Oink
30. Gestapo
32. Inept
33. Eventual
34. Stud

DOWN:
1. Handcuff
2. Nestbox
4. Anti
5. Ash
6. Lorry
7. Loss
8. Dye
11. Scorpion
13. Pawnshop
15. Edge
17. Lyre
18. Besotted
21. Oddment
24. Taste
26. Ogre
28. Iota
29. Kin
31. Aft

## Puzzle 25

**ACROSS:**
1. Tortoise
5. Gang
9. Pivot
10. Liaison
11. Alcove
12. Ennui
14. Try out
16. Warmth
19. Label
21. Ascend
24. Toecaps
25. Eerie
26. Cosy
27. Snapshot

**DOWN:**
1. Tops
2. Rivalry
3. Outdo
4. Spleen
6. Arson
7. Gunfight
8. Camera
13. Athletic
15. Unload
17. Monarch
18. Damson
20. Bless
22. Cheep
23. Seat

## Puzzle 26

**ACROSS:**
1. Cent
3. Stocking
9. Earnest
10. Users
11. V-neck
12. Obtain
14. Ginger
16. Eczema
19. Assign
21. Edict
24. Creel
25. Grinder
26. Regional
27. Easy

**DOWN:**
1. Cleavage
2. Nurse
4. Tattoo
5. Court
6. Itemize
7. Gush
8. Heckle
13. Masterly
15. Nest egg
17. Cleric
18. Enigma
20. Igloo
22. India
23. Scar

## Puzzle 27

**ACROSS:**
7. Rigour
8. Astray
9. Opus
10. Instruct
11. Slipper
13. Beard
15. Anger
17. Airship
20. Scissors
21. Toga
22. Warren
23. Excuse

**DOWN:**
1. Dispel
2. Toss
3. Trailer
4. Lapse
5. Starters
6. Cancer
12. Pressure
14. Tissues
16. Nectar
18. Ingest
19. Found
21. Tack

## Puzzle 28

**ACROSS:**
1. Satan
5. Pause
8. Erase
9. Noose
10. Alibi
11. Defer
12. Annoy
15. Lance
18. Old
20. Attend
21. Riyadh
22. Day
24. Chief
27. Tsars
30. Aorta
31. Realm
32. Pride
33. Elide
34. Emend
35. Rhyme

**DOWN:**
1. Santa
2. Thorn
3. Needy
4. Lawful
5. Pearl
6. Union
7. Elite
13. Notch
14. Obese
16. Abyss
17. Cider
18. Odd
19. Dry
23. Afraid
24. Carve
25. Irate
26. Famed
27. Taper
28. Amity
29. Siege

## Puzzle 29

**ACROSS:**
1. Bark
5. Fuss
7. Niagara
8. Rhetoric
10. Dust
12. Aged
14. Deranged
16. Leap-frog
17. Oath
18. Jeer
19. Sycamore
22. Ecuador
23. Fund
24. Troy

**DOWN:**
1. Boar
2. Knot
3. Labrador
4. Talc
5. Fandango
6. Sift
9. Hygiene
11. Shelter
13. Deported
15. Regicide
18. Jiff
19. Stub
20. Mart
21. Envy

## Puzzle 30

**ACROSS:**
1. Sabot
4. Meadow
9. Leaflet
10. Ibsen
11. Rode
12. Costume
13. Ark
14. Star
16. Rate
18. Boy
20. Capsule
21. Evil
24. Title
25. Salerno
26. Errata
27. Theme

**DOWN:**
1. Salary
2. Bland
3. Toll
5. Emissary
6. Disgust
7. Winter
8. Stick
13. Argument
15. Tipster
17. Scythe
18. Beast
19. Alcove
22. Verve
23. Blot

## Puzzle 31

ACROSS:
1. Vacant
4. Fatal
8. Nudge
9. Radiate
10. Tickled
11. Opie
12. Era
14. Glen
15. Base
18. Gag
21. Riot
23. Lantern
25. Pattern
26. Ascot
27. Lurid
28. Stolid

DOWN:
1. Vanity
2. Codicil
3. Needling
4. Fade
5. Tramp
6. Lieder
7. Bride
13. Abundant
16. Stencil
17. Propel
19. Gland
20. United
22. Otter
24. Vend

## Puzzle 32

ACROSS:
7. Sacred
8. French
10. Burnish
11. Waist
12. Reed
13. Cloak
17. Knees
18. Pair
22. Drool
23. Eclipse
24. Ornate
25. Stereo

DOWN:
1. Isobars
2. Scarlet
3. Genie
4. Crowbar
5. Untie
6. Chute
9. Sheltered
14. Inflate
15. Campari
16. Freedom
19. Idiom
20. Point
21. Blitz

## Puzzle 33

ACROSS:
1. Brute
4. Amidst
9. Lattice
10. Turin
11. Axel
12. Tornado
13. Coy
14. Omar
16. Auto
18. Awl
20. Radical
21. Poor
24. Naive
25. Gallant
26. Elapse
27. Ypres

DOWN:
1. Ballad
2. Untie
3. Edit
5. Maternal
6. Dormant
7. Tendon
8. Deity
13. Crickets
15. Madeira
17. Prince
18. Align
19. Brutus
22. On air
23. Ploy

## Puzzle 34

| ACROSS: | DOWN: |
|---|---|
| 7. Estate | 1. Tea leaf |
| 8. Rustle | 2. Eternal |
| 10. Larders | 3. Ether |
| 11. Ionia | 4. Auditor |
| 12. Arab | 5. Stand |
| 13. Arson | 6. Pedal |
| 17. Choke | 9. Astrakhan |
| 18. Star | 14. Chapter |
| 22. Clasp | 15. Strayed |
| 23. Animate | 16. Trieste |
| 24. Banter | 19. Scuba |
| 25. Repent | 20. Jaunt |
| | 21. Miser |

## Puzzle 35

| ACROSS: | DOWN: |
|---|---|
| 7. Vapour | 1. Damask |
| 8. Oracle | 2. Book |
| 9. Talk | 3. Trident |
| 10. Debonair | 4. Lobby |
| 11. Skating | 5. Magnetic |
| 13. Steep | 6. Plaice |
| 15. Razor | 12. Two-timer |
| 17. Brocade | 14. Trinket |
| 20. Taciturn | 16. Awaken |
| 21. Rare | 18. Duress |
| 22. Cement | 19. Lusty |
| 23. Emboss | 21. Ruby |

## Puzzle 36

| ACROSS: | DOWN: |
|---|---|
| 1. Sparse | 1. Sesame |
| 4. Gamble | 2. Awful |
| 9. Softest | 3. Seethed |
| 10. Inner | 5. Aries |
| 11. Mulch | 6. Bonjour |
| 12. Cassock | 7. Eureka |
| 13. Dead ringers | 8. Stick insect |
| 18. Airless | 14. Earlier |
| 20. Arise | 15. Ghastly |
| 22. Lying | 16. Ballet |
| 23. Cottage | 17. Redeem |
| 24. Target | 19. Eagle |
| 25. System | 21. Inapt |

## Puzzle 37

| ACROSS: | DOWN: |
|---|---|
| 1. Palisade | 1. Pipe |
| 5. Opus | 2. Lingo |
| 9. Pen name | 3. Spa |
| 11. Choir | 4. Duel |
| 12. Ally | 6. Problem |
| 14. Cot | 7. Sergeant |
| 16. Lee | 8. Icy |
| 18. Annotate | 10. Magnolia |
| 20. Bias | 13. Litigant |
| 22. Omen | 15. Task |
| 23. Skylight | 17. Obelisks |
| 24. Lei | 19. Tote |
| 25. Eft | 21. Asinine |
| 27. Barn | 26. Focus |
| 30. Snipe | 27. Bee |
| 31. Ethical | 28. Rein |
| 33. Shed | 29. Plea |
| 34. Undersea | 32. Hoe |

## Puzzle 38

| ACROSS: | DOWN: |
|---|---|
| 1. Shy | 1. Sparkler |
| 3. Negligent | 2. Yacht |
| 8. Ascertain | 3. Narwhal |
| 9. Urn | 4. Grasps |
| 10. Ketchup | 5. Inner |
| 11. Raid | 6. Elusive |
| 13. Edible | 7. Tent |
| 15. Career | 12. Gradient |
| 18. Died | 14. Idiotic |
| 20. Parched | 16. Airport |
| 23. Nut | 17. Opaque |
| 24. Liquorice | 19. Delta |
| 25. Bucharest | 21. Haifa |
| 26. Act | 22. Snub |

## Puzzle 39

| ACROSS: | DOWN: |
|---|---|
| 1. Apple | 1. Above |
| 5. Force | 2. Peril |
| 8. Rural | 3. Errs |
| 9. Oar | 4. Area |
| 10. Annoy | 5. Flak |
| 11. Smack | 6. Ran |
| 14. Eels | 7. Egypt |
| 17. Mast | 12. Magenta |
| 19. Algebra | 13. Cabaret |
| 20. Bill | 15. Evict |
| 21. Gear | 16. Salty |
| 22. Tantrum | 17. Magma |
| 23. Stay | 18. Scale |
| 24. Abel | 23. Sober |
| 27. Facts | 25. Bible |
| 30. Bingo | 26. Ladle |
| 32. Bad | 27. Foal |
| 33. Acrid | 28. Card |
| 34. Rebel | 29. Suds |
| 35. Scene | 31. Nib |

## Puzzle 40

ACROSS:
1. Large
5. Franc
8. Viral
9. Apt
10. Audio
11. Nippy
14. Took
17. Loch
19. Ensnarl
20. Hart
21. Awry
22. Calcium
23. Pith
24. Apse
27. Erato
30. Again
32. Awe
33. Valve
34. Husky
35. Night

DOWN:
1. Least
2. Ratio
3. Even
4. Crop
5. Flay
6. Add
7. Cloth
12. Insular
13. Pianist
15. Okapi
16. Ketch
17. Llama
18. Corps
23. Poach
25. Prang
26. Event
27. Envy
28. Able
29. Omen
31. Ass

## Puzzle 41

ACROSS:
1. Saga
3. Calmest
9. Massacred
10. Ode
11. Ruby
13. Snicker
15. Anther
17. Canine
19. Curtail
20. Apex
22. Dun
23. Organised
25. Hearing
26. Spin

DOWN:
1. Same
2. Gas
4. Across
5. Madeira
6. Stockpile
7. Baby
8. Learner
12. Utterance
14. Bar code
16. Enamour
18. Flagon
20. Acne
21. Aden
24. Sap

## Puzzle 42

ACROSS:
1. Crying
4. Martyr
9. Occur
10. Renal
11. Tease
12. Catch
14. Essay
16. Red
18. Alpha
19. Image
21. Pop
24. Water
27. Admit
29. Unite
30. Prior
31. Satin
32. Deeply
33. Speech

DOWN:
1. Crouch
2. Yacht
3. North
5. Agree
6. Tongs
7. Relays
8. Abate
13. Copse
15. Stand
16. Rap
17. Dip
20. Swiped
22. Ovine
23. Stench
25. Tribe
26. Rural
27. Aesop
28. Metre

## Puzzle 43

| ACROSS: | DOWN: |
|---------|-------|
| 1. Amazon | 1. Almond |
| 4. Arthur | 2. Annul |
| 9. Mince | 3. Ocean |
| 10. Bevel | 5. Rebec |
| 11. Abode | 6. Hover |
| 12. Nylon | 7. Relief |
| 14. Carve | 8. Snout |
| 16. Ate | 13. Oasis |
| 18. Miser | 15. Ankle |
| 19. Waken | 16. Are |
| 21. Eve | 17. Ewe |
| 24. Amass | 20. Tarmac |
| 27. Seams | 22. Verse |
| 29. Arrow | 23. Astern |
| 30. Maori | 25. Agony |
| 31. Exile | 26. Saint |
| 32. Coyote | 27. Sweep |
| 33. Option | 28. Alibi |

## Puzzle 44

| ACROSS: | DOWN: |
|---------|-------|
| 1. Coalition | 1. Cubicle |
| 6. Tom | 2. Angle |
| 8. Bogus | 3. Inserted |
| 9. Fencing | 4. Influx |
| 10. Cheerful | 5. None |
| 11. Soot | 6. Tripoli |
| 13. Easier | 7. Might |
| 15. Sprint | 12. Approach |
| 18. Bank | 14. Sunrise |
| 19. Garrison | 16. Tonight |
| 22. Arizona | 17. Safari |
| 23. Among | 18. Brawl |
| 24. Lee | 20. Scone |
| 25. Brightest | 21. Bomb |

## Puzzle 45

| ACROSS: | DOWN: |
|---------|-------|
| 1. Dagger | 1. Damage |
| 4. Savage | 2. Gnu |
| 7. Sunflower | 3. Refinery |
| 9. Axe | 4. Slow |
| 10. Urn | 5. Vie |
| 11. Ink | 6. Eggnog |
| 14. Eden | 7. Selection |
| 15. Enticing | 8. Ruminated |
| 17. Tread | 12. Knead |
| 18. Betrayal | 13. Kid |
| 19. Lamb | 16. Talisman |
| 21. Dim | 17. Tax |
| 22. Leo | 18. Belong |
| 24. Ear | 20. Burrow |
| 25. Nursemaid | 23. Asia |
| 28. Geneva | 26. Use |
| 29. Nephew | 27. Imp |

## Puzzle 46

**ACROSS:**
1. Thawed
4. Drying
7. Bracelets
9. Ear
10. Urn
11. Use
14. Dead
15. Incident
17. Wotan
18. Bed-linen
19. Oslo
21. Rod
22. Raw
24. Dot
25. Negotiate
28. Warmer
29. Eleven

**DOWN:**
1. Thread
2. War
3. Decision
4. Doll
5. Yet
6. Garnet
7. Breakdown
8. Supersede
12. Enter
13. Gin
16. Canonize
17. Wig
18. Barrow
20. Obtain
23. Poor
26. Elm
27. Tee

## Puzzle 47

**ACROSS:**
1. Cognac
4. Equate
8. Gauge
10. Elver
11. Amass
12. Emend
14. Talon
16. One
18. Ever
19. Veal
21. Ewe
24. Could
27. Umber
29. Recur
30. Igloo
31. Bully
32. Tether
33. Answer

**DOWN:**
1. Cygnet
2. Gouge
3. Ahead
5. Quest
6. Anvil
7. Errand
9. Warn
13. Novel
15. Alarm
16. Ore
17. Eve
20. Script
22. Wick
23. Prayer
25. Unlit
26. Drone
27. Urban
28. Below

## Puzzle 48

**ACROSS:**
1. Prompt
5. Scampi
8. Open
9. Shackled
10. Slyly
11. Heedful
14. Bidder
15. Garish
17. Feasted
19. Annoy
21. Jubilant
23. Weld
24. Bereft
25. Malady

**DOWN:**
2. Repulsive
3. Mingled
4. Task
5. Scavenge
6. Asked
7. Pie
12. Unspoiled
13. Artefact
16. Renewal
18. Seize
20. Stem
22. Use

## Puzzle 49

ACROSS:
1. Encrypt
5. Watts
8. Née
9. Diploma
10. Sieve
11. Dot
13. Nullified
15. Strive
17. Prefer
20. Obbligato
21. Lay
23. Dairy
25. Interim
26. Own
27. Ascot
28. Applaud

DOWN:
1. Egdod
2. Cipot
3. Yrotnevni
4. Tnailp
5. Wes
6. Tseriaf
7. Sserder
12. Oot
14. Irruop-top
15. Suoudra
16. Rebmilc
18. Ela
19. Lamina
21. Lirpa
22. Ymmud
24. Yot

## Puzzle 50

ACROSS:
1. Zebra
3. Beatles
6. Reduced
8. Larva
10. Flamboyance
12. Hare
13. Aside
15. Cell
17. Battlefield
19. Cadet
20. Chicken
21. Sextant
22. Merge

DOWN:
1. Zurich
2. Rouble
3. Bad
4. Tiara
5. Scared
7. Enmeshed
9. Goldfish
10. Front
11. Naked
14. Abacus
15. Cliche
16. Lounge
18. Treat
20. Cat

## Puzzle 51

ACROSS:
1. Joker
3. Chapter
6. Radiant
8. Antic
10. Complicated
12. Near
13. Alley
15. Taps
17. Bank-holiday
19. Eager
20. Skittle
21. Tartare
22. Acute

DOWN:
1. Jargon
2. Editor
3. Cat
4. Panda
5. Recede
7. Napoleon
9. Limerick
10. Cabin
11. Today
14. Absent
15. Tactic
16. Scheme
18. Knelt
20. She

## Puzzle 52

**ACROSS:**
1. Price
4. Earnest
7. Easter
10. Idol
12. Beast
13. Lease
14. Rim
15. Etch
16. Picador
19. Mascot
20. Voices
23. Stretch
25. Bald
27. Lad
28. Motet
29. Gnats
31. Gust
32. Divest
33. Tardily
34. Mimic

**DOWN:**
1. Problem
2. Idea
3. East
4. Eyelid
5. Noise
6. Tilth
8. Aspic
9. Removed
11. Detach
14. Rattled
16. Psalms
17. Cos
18. Rot
21. Icons
22. Seismic
24. Ratify
25. Bigot
26. Doted
29. Germ
30. Atom

## Puzzle 53

**ACROSS:**
7. Twelve
8. Archer
9. Reroute
10. Erie
11. Tennyson
13. Doll
14. Host
16. Allergic
18. Mail
20. Catarrh
22. Turtle
23. Noodle

**DOWN:**
1. Swerve
2. Clarinet
3. Menu
4. Maternal
5. Acne
6. Aerial
12. Searched
13. Darkroom
15. Opaque
17. Inhale
19. Late
21. Tent

## Puzzle 54

**ACROSS:**
1. Gash
3. Improper
9. Nictate
10. Metre
11. Misde-
    meanour
13. Tremor
15. Stoker
17. Consecration
20. Alive
21. Chemise
22. Sinister
23. Imps

**DOWN:**
1. Gunsmith
2. Socks
4. Meeker
5. Remonstrated
6. Pot luck
7. Reek
8. Ravenousness
12. Princess
14. Erosion
16. Icicle
18. Idiom
19. Mass

## Puzzle 55

**ACROSS:**
7. Kennel
8. Azalea
9. Eggheads
10. Acid
11. Hear
12. Identify
14. Airtight
17. Also
19. Bomb
20. Accident
21. Camera
22. Nickel

**DOWN:**
1. Beagle
2. Anchor
3. Cleaning
4. Bass
5. Vacant
6. Belief
13. Enticing
15. Isobar
16. Tablet
17. Abduct
18. Singer
20. Away

## Puzzle 56

**ACROSS:**
7. Marina
8. Halted
9. Epic
10. Lifeboat
11. Adamant
13. Begin
15. Paces
16. Baggage
18. Somewhat
19. Sash
21. Falcon
22. Rueful

**DOWN:**
1. Warp
2. Circumfer-
   ence
3. Garland
4. Shift
5. Flabbergasted
6. Relaxing
12. Diagonal
14. Battery
17. Think
20. Shun

## Puzzle 57

**ACROSS:**
1. Shy
3. Cascading
8. Ascertain
9. Map
10. Lettuce
11. Yard
13. Sanity
15. Tavern
18. Aged
20. Implode
23. Use
24. Imitation
25. Satellite
26. Get

**DOWN:**
1. Smallest
2. Yacht
3. Circuit
4. Scared
5. Annoy
6. Immerse
7. Gape
12. Internet
14. Neglect
16. Appease
17. Bikini
19. Drill
21. Owing
22. Fuss

## Puzzle 58

ACROSS:
1. Factory
4. Demon
7. Safer
10. Label
11. Owl
12. Ayr
13. Decay
14. Eager
16. Bottle
18. Active
22. Stair
24. Cheap
26. Zoo
27. Art
28. Lobby
29. Igloo
31. Daddy
32. Neptune

DOWN:
1. Fused
2. Toe
3. Yelled
4. Debug
5. Molar
6. Narrate
8. Facet
9. Royal
15. Eat
16. Buzzard
17. Tot
19. Cacti
20. Ideal
21. Crayon
22. Solid
23. Abbey
25. Probe
30. Gut

## Puzzle 59

ACROSS:
1. Joint
4. Brigand
8. Lasso
9. Operate
10. Illness
11. Emend
12. Yarrow
14. Iguana
18. Thief
20. Empathy
22. Toecaps
23. Photo
24. Residue
25. Lisle

DOWN:
1. Jollity
2. Insular
3. Trove
4. Biopsy
5. Iceberg
6. Agate
7. Dread
13. Offhand
15. Actions
16. Anymore
17. Lessee
18. Tutor
19. Items
21. Papal

## Puzzle 60

ACROSS:
1. Sparse
4. Elapse
8. India
10. Climb
11. Scone
12. Girth
14. Surly
16. Elf
18. Pine
19. Echo
21. Low
24. Beige
27. Grass
29. Ruler
30. Ounce
31. Agile
32. Gyrate
33. Genius

DOWN:
1. Stingy
2. Adder
3. Slash
5. Laces
6. Prior
7. Embryo
9. Boil
13. Thing
15. Usher
16. Eel
17. Few
20. Oblong
22. Oily
23. Assess
25. Inner
26. Erect
27. Grape
28. Alibi

## Puzzle 61

**ACROSS:**
1. Accent
4. Method
8. Toast
10. Tempt
11. Elder
12. Aphid
14. Adder
16. Aye
18. Apex
19. Read
21. Eta
24. Adult
27. Death
29. Aster
30. Exits
31. Alien
32. Yanked
33. Canine

**DOWN:**
1. Actual
2. Coach
3. Noted
5. Extra
6. Humid
7. Deters
9. Edgy
13. Impel
15. Drake
16. Axe
17. Era
20. Bakery
22. Tate
23. Chance
25. Union
26. Taste
27. Drama
28. Alibi

## Puzzle 62

**ACROSS:**
7. Sextet
8. Twiggy
10. Riotous
11. Where
12. Noel
13. Beard
17. Globe
18. Bent
22. Islam
23. Earthen
24. Anoint
25. Scarab

**DOWN:**
1. G-string
2. Exposed
3. Lemon
4. Awkward
5. Ogres
6. Lycee
9. Assembled
14. Aliment
15. Leghorn
16. Stand-by
19. Vicar
20. Allot
21. Trice

## Puzzle 63

**ACROSS:**
1. Chump
4. Topical
8. Shotgun
9. Druid
10. Astra
11. Eclipse
13. Nero
15. Karate
17. Ousted
20. Lips
22. Against
24. Ultra
26. Patch
27. Lapwing
28. Endemic
29. Ruled

**DOWN:**
1. Cossack
2. U-boat
3. Pageant
4. Tender
5. Pedal
6. Crumpet
7. Lodge
12. Coop
14. Eels
16. Reacted
18. Usurper
19. Dragged
21. Italic
22. Ample
23. Nahum
25. Trill

## Puzzle 64

**ACROSS:**
1. Virago
7. Macabre
8. Gangster
9. Stand
10. Routs
11. Cool
12. Melee
15. Hence
16. Siena
19. Aver
20. Facet
21. Ochre
22. Reveller
23. Imposes
24. Mystic

**DOWN:**
1. Vigorous
2. Renounce
3. Gusts
4. Car
5. Tattle
6. France
7. Mercenaries
9. Some
13. Lancelot
14. Esoteric
15. Have
17. Income
18. Narrow
20. Fiery
22. Rex

## Puzzle 65

**ACROSS:**
1. Mart
5. East
7. Eyeball
8. Deadlock
10. Gory
12. Used
14. Easiness
16. Slag heap
17. Etui
18. Ante
19. Ephemera
22. Ego-trip
23. Maul
24. Edgy

**DOWN:**
1. Maid
2. Tend
3. Kerosene
4. Pack
5. Elegance
6. Tiny
9. Epsilon
11. Rescuer
13. Doggerel
15. Sapphire
18. Adam
19. Eyot
20. Mope
21. Army

## Puzzle 66

**ACROSS:**
4. Delude
5. Thus
7. Cajoled
10. Utter
11. Disrupt
12. Sorry
14. Titbits
15. Greet
16. Deplore
20. Avoid
21. Estates
22. Loud
23. Callow

**DOWN:**
1. Flood
2. Edges
3. Ghettos
4. Dear
6. Sherry
8. Limited
9. Dribble
10. Upstart
13. Grovel
14. Tedious
17. Oscar
18. Eagle
19. Meow

## Puzzle 67

**ACROSS:**
1. School
7. Apostle
8. Language
9. Dance
10. Truce
11. Leap
12. Weird
15. Cumin
16. Yodel
19. Lair
20. Spoor
21. Denim
22. Atlantic
23. Ellipse
24. Belles

**DOWN:**
1. Salutary
2. Honoured
3. Ovule
4. Ape
5. Escape
6. Slicer
7. Agglomerate
9. Dawn
13. Immortal
14. Derricks
15. Clam
17. Overly
18. Elicit
20. Shale
22. Asp

## Puzzle 68

**ACROSS:**
1. Jackal
4. Brest
8. Split
9. Airship
10. Expired
11. Acyl
12. Yet
14. Soho
15. Alps
18. Red
21. Eels
23. Extract
25. Avocado
26. First
27. Rhyme
28. Sleeve

**DOWN:**
1. Jester
2. Calypso
3. Anterior
4. Burr
5. Ethic
6. Tipple
7. Dandy
13. Tasteful
16. Prairie
17. Repair
19. Defoe
20. Statue
22. Loony
24. Dame

## Puzzle 69

**ACROSS:**
1. Wallet
4. Width
8. Amour
9. Rainbow
10. Overlap
11. Ugli
12. Tar
14. Isle
15. Eden
18. Dis
21. Lint
23. Oak-tree
25. Mafiosi
26. Evens
27. Style
28. Isatin

**DOWN:**
1. Weapon
2. Lioness
3. Enrolled
4. Wait
5. Debug
6. Hawaii
7. Crypt
13. Reckless
16. Earnest
17. Plumes
19. Sonic
20. Lessen
22. Nifty
24. Mope

## Puzzle 70

| ACROSS: | DOWN: |
|---|---|
| 1. Khaki | 2. Halve |
| 4. T-bone | 3. Keynote |
| 10. Relayed | 5. Banal |
| 11. Noisy | 6. Nairobi |
| 12. Credo | 7. Truck |
| 13. Eelworm | 8. Idler |
| 15. Tart | 9. Pygmy |
| 17. Agree | 14. Eton |
| 19. Oasis | 16. Aeon |
| 22. Owns | 18. Garment |
| 25. Airline | 20. Ashamed |
| 27. Haste | 21. Sable |
| 29. Liege | 23. Weedy |
| 30. Damping | 24. Merge |
| 31. State | 26. Inert |
| 32. Adult | 28. Swirl |

## Puzzle 71

| ACROSS: | DOWN: |
|---|---|
| 1. Focus | 1. Filched |
| 4. Spangle | 2. Clamp |
| 8. Cup | 3. Scar |
| 9. Llama | 4. Spot |
| 10. Scant | 5. Also |
| 11. Ratio | 6. Grass |
| 14. Hope | 7. Enter |
| 16. User | 12. Airline |
| 18. Arrived | 13. Invoice |
| 19. Dabs | 15. Easel |
| 21. Deaf | 16. Udder |
| 23. Edifice | 17. Era |
| 24. Well | 20. Age |
| 26. Rags | 22. Fashion |
| 28. Beset | 24. Watch |
| 31. Tiara | 25. Leant |
| 32. Alibi | 27. Agile |
| 33. Nun | 28. Bath |
| 34. Hatched | 29. Send |
| 35. Glean | 30. Tang |

## Puzzle 72

| ACROSS: | DOWN: |
|---|---|
| 1. Teenager | 1. Taut |
| 5. Iced | 2. Emits |
| 8. Uniforms | 3. Apologetic |
| 9. Alms | 4. Elm |
| 11. Show-stopper | 6. Calypso |
| 14. Era | 7. Disorder |
| 16. Erica | 10. Howard Keel |
| 17. Ore | 12. Shiva |
| 18. Reprimanded | 13. Fearsome |
| 21. Ogre | 15. Apparel |
| 22. Reveller | 19. Delve |
| 24. Eels | 20. Troy |
| 25. Adultery | 23. End |

## Puzzle 73

**ACROSS:**
1. Aghast
4. Critic
7. Assure
9. Sent
11. Bat
12. Euro
13. Damsel
14. Eyrie
16. Diva
17. Size
18. Roast
21. Hearse
23. Pore
25. Use
26. Odds
27. Scythe
29. Rotund
30. Sleazy

**DOWN:**
1. Award
2. Has
3. Treble
4. Castor
5. Tutu
6. Calorie
8. Unscarred
10. Necessary
15. Yes
16. Despair
19. Amused
20. Thesis
22. Every
24. Rout
28. Tea

## Puzzle 74

**ACROSS:**
7. Nearly
8. Island
9. Lenience
10. Bid
11. Insignia
13. Cool
14. Each
16. Mattress
18. Inn
19. Antonyms
22. Cygnet
23. Bonded

**DOWN:**
1. Ceylon
2. Brandish
3. Byre
4. Aircraft
5. Fly
6. Indigo
12. Nominate
13. Carrying
15. Annoys
17. Sussex
20. Orbs
21. End

## Puzzle 75

**ACROSS:**
3. Ago
7. Orders
8. Bamboo
9. Beverage
10. Adam
11. Seal
12. Sparkled
15. Prisoner
18. Sane
20. Wade
21. Bordeaux
22. Career
23. Failed
24. Kit

**DOWN:**
1. Freeze
2. Repeal
3. Assassin
4. Oboe
5. Embark
6. Rotate
11. Sap
13. Aircraft
14. Dye
16. Reagan
17. Skewer
18. Scenic
19. Nausea
21. Bark

## Puzzle 76

**ACROSS:**
7. Target
8. Avenge
9. Bluebell
10. Said
11. Stud
12. Gruesome
15. Crotchet
18. Same
20. Spur
21. Sombrero
22. Carols
23. Tiptoe

**DOWN:**
1. Ballot
2. Agreed
3. Strength
4. Ball
5. Census
6. Egoism
11. Sac
13. Ultimate
14. Eke
16. Repeat
17. Terror
18. Scrape
19. Marrow
21. Sash

## Puzzle 77

**ACROSS:**
7. Coaxed
8. Novice
9. Magi
10. Asteroid
11. Manicure
13. Mate
14. Taxi
16. Sardinia
18. Fountain
20. Inns
21. Hassle
22. Squirm

**DOWN:**
1. Sonata
2. Exhibitionist
3. Idea
4. Knitwear
5. Over ambitious
6. Script
12. Unshaven
15. Amoral
17. Ignore
19. Nose

## Puzzle 78

**ACROSS:**
7. Parcel
8. Idlest
9. Sari
10. Molecule
11. Freezing
13. Numb
14. Edit
16. Aperitif
18. Narrator
20. Ease
21. Borneo
22. Sherry

**DOWN:**
1. Bazaar
2. Accident-prone
3. Glum
4. Dialogue
5. Ill-considered
6. Asylum
12. Inaction
15. Dragon
17. Insert
19. Rase

## Puzzle 79

| ACROSS: | DOWN: |
|---|---|
| 7. Health | 1. Decide |
| 8. Either | 2. Blooms |
| 9. Dinosaur | 3. Shrapnel |
| 10. Away | 4. Bear |
| 11. News | 5. Ottawa |
| 12. Nictated | 6. Female |
| 14. Miracles | 13. Cassette |
| 17. Amen | 15. Isobar |
| 19. Gold | 16. Andrew |
| 20. Predator | 17. Azalea |
| 21. Career | 18. Evolve |
| 22. Twelve | 20. Port |

## Puzzle 80

| ACROSS: | DOWN: |
|---|---|
| 1. Kirsch | 1. Kiosk |
| 4. Sahara | 2. Rue |
| 7. Ocelot | 3. Hatred |
| 9. Sick | 4. System |
| 11. Rat | 5. Asks |
| 12. Oslo | 6. Acrobat |
| 13. Kettle | 8. Letter-box |
| 14. Demur | 10. Courteous |
| 16. Safe | 15. Eke |
| 17. Tuft | 16. Satanic |
| 18. Romeo | 19. Misery |
| 21. Utopia | 20. Outfit |
| 23. Also | 22. Atlas |
| 25. Sit | 24. Sane |
| 26. Axle | 28. Sir |
| 27. Fossil | |
| 29. Cheeky | |
| 30. Taurus | |

## Puzzle 81

| ACROSS: | DOWN: |
|---|---|
| 7. Ballet | 1. Casket |
| 8. Isobar | 2. Blending |
| 9. Kindest | 3. Stye |
| 10. Late | 4. Fiftieth |
| 11. Attitude | 5. Boil |
| 13. Sank | 6. Canton |
| 14. Slug | 12. Unending |
| 16. Exhaling | 13. Solecism |
| 18. Ogle | 15. Lagoon |
| 20. Debacle | 17. Needle |
| 22. Jordan | 19. Eddy |
| 23. Nestle | 21. Band |

## Puzzle 82

**ACROSS:**
1. Kipper
4. Rungs
8. Aesop
9. Samovar
10. Enamour
11. Flan
12. Yen
14. Kepi
15. Amos
18. Air
21. Rice
23. Archway
25. Embargo
26. Shrub
27. Toady
28. Tinsel

**DOWN:**
1. Knaves
2. Passage
3. Euphoria
4. Romp
5. Novel
6. Sarong
7. Usury
13. Narcissi
16. Onwards
17. Priest
19. Razor
20. Cymbal
22. Cobra
24. Orgy

## Puzzle 83

**ACROSS:**
7. Oddity
8. Arable
10. Halogen
11. Sheen
12. Rise
13. Dummy
17. Gifts
18. Thor
22. Orang
23. Olympus
24. Cannon
25. Proton

**DOWN:**
1. Yoghurt
2. Idolise
3. Stage
4. Irksome
5. Ebbed
6. Penny
9. Intuition
14. Widgeon
15. Chapati
16. Erasing
19. Pooch
20. Nanny
21. Hydro

## Puzzle 84

**ACROSS:**
1. Zebra
4. Dhobi
10. Dropper
11. Alone
12. Hyena
13. Pastime
15. Eden
17. Viola
19. Tonga
22. Lair
25. Enliven
27. Couch
29. Semis
30. Scarper
31. Ocean
32. Adorn

**DOWN:**
2. Erode
3. Raphael
5. Heaps
6. Booking
7. Idaho
8. Grope
9. Genes
14. Anti
16. Dale
18. Islamic
20. Orchard
21. Tease
23. Angst
24. Shorn
26. Vista
28. Upper

## Puzzle 85

**ACROSS:**
1. Sailor
4. Clerk
8. Holed
9. Admired
10. Regrets
11. Clue
12. Ado
14. Plot
15. Bark
18. She
21. Hobo
23. Beeline
25. Persian
26. Voice
27. Niece
28. Dragon

**DOWN:**
1. Sahara
2. Illegal
3. Oddments
4. Coma
5. Enrol
6. Kidney
7. Balsa
13. Observer
16. Raising
17. Chopin
19. Ebony
20. Demean
22. Barge
24. Dire

## Puzzle 86

**ACROSS:**
1. Veer
5. Ring
7. Invoice
8. Tattered
10. Cash
12. Espy
14. Inspired
16. Peerless
17. Neil
18. Oslo
19. Credible
22. Treason
23. Etch
24. Sort

**DOWN:**
1. Vest
2. Riot
3. Override
4. Kind
5. Reaction
6. Gush
9. Answers
11. Special
13. Yarmouth
15. Suspense
18. Ooze
19. Crew
20. Ions
21. Emit

## Puzzle 87

**ACROSS:**
7. Advert
8. Inside
10. Offence
11. Bloom
12. Carp
13. Began
17. Junta
18. Keep
22. Thumb
23. Absolve
24. Coffee
25. Placid

**DOWN:**
1. Majorca
2. Oviform
3. Bring
4. Antbear
5. Bigot
6. Beams
9. Celestial
14. Bubbled
15. Wedlock
16. Appends
19. Stack
20. Ruffs
21. Psalm

## Puzzle 88

**ACROSS:**
1. Dummy
4. Actors
9. Library
10. Outre
11. Axle
12. Impeach
13. Roc
14. Oboe
16. Nuke
18. Bug
20. Chuckle
21. Jamb
24. Cadre
25. Naivety
26. Egress
27. Cited

**DOWN:**
1. Dallas
2. Mabel
3. Year
5. Chopping
6. Outback
7. Seethe
8. Cynic
13. Reckless
15. Blunder
17. Icicle
18. Beans
19. Obeyed
22. Alert
23. Zinc

## Puzzle 89

**ACROSS:**
1. Beleaguer
6. Mambo
9. Dogma
10. Gelignite
11. Dutchman
12. Access
14. Troy
15. Derivation
18. Metallurgy
19. Pyre
21. Linear
23. Self-help
26. Potpourri
27. Ingot
28. Eased
29. Evergreen

**DOWN:**
1. Boded
2. Lights out
3. Apathy
4. Ungraceful
5. Rely
6. Magician
7. Moire
8. Obeisance
13. Single file
14. Time-lapse
16. Ivy league
17. Alkaloid
20. Offing
22. Notes
24. Paten
25. Free

## Puzzle 90

**ACROSS:**
1. Rabble
7. Butcher
8. Quagmire
9. Miner
10. Ingot
11. Knob
12. Tepid
15. Punch
16. Ditty
19. Urge
20. Faint
21. Flare
22. Fracture
23. Inhabit
24. Stress

**DOWN:**
1. Required
2. Braggart
3. Limit
4. Hue
5. Scribe
6. Yemeni
7. Broken heart
9. Moth
13. Pedicure
14. Deftness
15. Pyre
17. Island
18. Turban
20. Facet
22. Fir

## Puzzle 91

ACROSS:
7. Ernest
8. Dotage
10. Largess
11. Crest
12. Cost
13. Faced
17. Baulk
18. Bade
22. Array
23. Sporran
24. Tissue
25. Banker

DOWN:
1. Hemlock
2. Encrust
3. Usher
4. Voucher
5. Eager
6. Yeats
9. Establish
14. Papyrus
15. Paprika
16. Deanery
19. Paste
20. Brisk
21. Moral

## Puzzle 92

ACROSS:
7. Canape
8. Barber
9. Beverage
10. Clan
11. Boat
13. Abdicate
15. Shrivels
17. Ease
19. Hint
20. Sardinia
22. Cheese
23. Scorch

DOWN:
1. Gazebo
2. Bare
3. Separate
4. Able
5. Tricycle
6. Decant
12. Thirteen
14. Distress
16. Height
18. Switch
20. Seek
21. Iron

## Puzzle 93

ACROSS:
1. Labour
5. Amused
8. Stye
9. Cadillac
10. Acrid
11. Ecstasy
14. Fickle
15. Tactic
17. Against
19. Brawl
21. Astonish
23. Area
24. Enzyme
25. Cheeky

DOWN:
2. Attaching
3. Obelisk
4. Race
5. Abdicate
6. Unlit
7. Era
12. Shipwreck
13. Perspire
16. Carnage
18. Irony
20. Chic
22. Son

## Puzzle 94

ACROSS:
1. Default
5. Award
8. Cobbler
9. Plays
10. Siege
11. Opening
12. Clouts
14. Judges
17. Blender
19. Rapid
22. Aware
23. Hygiene
24. Exert
25. Rotated

DOWN:
1. Ducks
2. Fable
3. Ugliest
4. Terror
5. Apple
6. Amazing
7. Designs
12. Cabbage
13. Operate
15. Upright
16. Archer
18. Dwelt
20. Pleat
21. Dread

## Puzzle 95

ACROSS:
1. Forlorn
4. Basis
7. Radio
10. Aorta
11. Van
12. Cat
13. Exude
14. Chalk
16. Ghetto
18. Uneven
22. Comma
24. Split
26. Moa
27. Pit
28. Trick
29. Yeast
31. Tarot
32. Numeral

DOWN:
1. Force
2. Lei
3. Nuance
4. Burma
5. Shack
6. Section
8. Deuce
9. Overt
15. Lee
16. Garment
17. Too
19. Nasty
20. Villa
21. Napkin
22. Cater
23. Moist
25. Total
30. Eke

## Puzzle 96

ACROSS:
2. Badge
5. Abate
8. Ado
9. Nectarine
11. Naked
12. Earnestly
15. Credit
16. Billet
18. Defendant
21. Enter
22. Truncheon
24. Vat
25. Admit
26. Scene

DOWN:
1. Paint
2. Bookshelf
3. Dandelion
4. Escort
6. Burns
7. Tan
10. Egypt
13. Existence
14. Talkative
15. Cadet
17. Caress
19. Ennui
20. Broth
23. Rid

## Puzzle 97

**ACROSS:**
1. Parcel
4. Quiche
9. Rampage
10. Hates
11. Style
12. Carnage
13. Crystallise
18. Cracked
20. Uncle
22. Extra
23. Saddens
24. Scream
25. Myopia

**DOWN:**
1. Peruse
2. Rummy
3. Erasers
5. Usher
6. Cutlass
7. Ensued
8. Merchandise
14. Reactor
15. Laundry
16. Access
17. Persia
19. Koala
21. Cheap

## Puzzle 98

**ACROSS:**
1. Sat
3. Carry
8. Retract
9. Polka
10. Maple
11. Undoing
12. Target
14. Nugget
18. Capable
20. Incur
22. Exist
23. Emotion
24. Enemy
25. Man

**DOWN:**
1. Set up
2. Trapeze
3. Citrus
4. Rapid
5. Yelling
6. Slang
7. Prompt
13. Reptile
15. Uniform
16. Throne
17. Celery
18. Creep
19. Bathe
21. Cairn

## Puzzle 99

**ACROSS:**
1. Nearby
4. Baboon
8. Grime
10. Bleep
11. Vital
12. Trite
14. Ennui
16. Bat
18. Logo
19. Arid
21. Wag
24. Tepee
27. Syrup
29. Lotto
30. Adieu
31. Lapse
32. Turkey
33. Prayer

**DOWN:**
1. Negate
2. Alibi
3. Breve
5. Amble
6. Ocean
7. Napkin
9. Etna
13. Those
15. Noisy
16. Bow
17. Tag
20. Strait
22. Alto
23. Appear
25. Prior
26. Elude
27. Solar
28. Ropey

## Puzzle 100

**ACROSS:**
2. Scald
4. Driftwood
6. Icarus
8. Samson
10. Pluck
11. Beacon
12. Bitten
13. Scans
15. Coffee
16. Tenure
18. Yorkshire
19. Their

**DOWN:**
1. Health
2. Slip up
3. Dvorak
4. Dragonfly
5. Disfigure
6. Isaac
7. Slice
8. Scant
9. Nitre
13. Secret
14. Senior
17. Asleep

## Puzzle 101

**ACROSS:**
1. Nation
4. Try out
7. Astronaut
9. Psi
10. Ass
11. Hop
14. Rill
15. Wastrels
17. Tepee
18. Cascaded
19. Hoof
21. Rag
22. Eel
24. Mad
25. Yuletides
28. Bounty
29. Elapse

**DOWN:**
1. Nipper
2. Ins
3. Narrowed
4. Tuna
5. You
6. Twists
7. Aimlessly
8. Tapeworms
12. Paper
13. Ate
16. Sedative
17. Tap
18. Cherub
20. Fiddle
23. Defy
26. Urn
27. Ena

## Puzzle 102

**ACROSS:**
1. Grovel
4. Bright
9. Persuaded
11. Ill
12. Gin
13. Usual
15. Ego
16. And
18. Atoll
19. Elope
21. Law
24. Aim
26. Begin
28. Air
29. Hut
30. Aeroplane
33. Simper
34. Sextet

**DOWN:**
1. Gypsum
2. Oar
3. Emu
5. Ridge
6. Guinea pig
7. Tallow
8. Adorn
10. Spa
14. Ultimatum
16. All
17. Dew
20. Pathos
22. Abort
23. Infect
25. Brace
27. Eel
31. Pie
32. Act

## Puzzle 103

**ACROSS:**
1. Look
3. Carousel
9. Viaduct
10. Solar
11. Neighbouring
13. Ermine
15. Scheme
17. Artificially
20. Alibi
21. Tendril
22. Tricycle
23. Weed

**DOWN:**
1. Lavender
2. Okapi
4. Action
5. Obstructions
6. Silence
7. Lurk
8. Authenticity
12. Recycled
14. Martini
16. Lintel
18. Large
19. Bait

## Puzzle 104

**ACROSS:**
1. Lathe
4. Seventy
7. Alibi
8. Coypu
10. Nun
11. Coo
12. Kayak
14. Clang
15. Yellow
18. Magnum
22. Rabbi
23. Beast
26. Via
27. Use
28. Abate
30. Crest
31. Harness
32. Dirty

**DOWN:**
1. Laundry
2. Thank
3. Edify
4. Sticky
5. Ego
6. Young
8. Cocoa
9. Yearn
13. Ail
16. Libra
17. Olive
19. Gas
20. Modesty
21. Abacus
22. Reach
24. Ahead
25. Tutor
29. Tan

## Puzzle 105

**ACROSS:**
1. Keg
3. Flash
8. Banjo
9. Angered
10. Abdomen
11. Banal
12. Number
14. Fascia
18. Bijou
20. Sabbath
22. Codeine
23. Oasis
24. Dread
25. Tic

**DOWN:**
1. Kingdom
2. Gloom
3. Flaunt
4. Algebra
5. Heron
6. Pedal
7. Obtain
13. Erudite
15. Classic
16. Aghast
17. Ascend
18. Bacon
19. Jaded
21. Boost

## Puzzle 106

**ACROSS:**
1. Diamond
5. Sabre
8. Leads
9. Skittle
10. Era
11. Insistent
13. Ritual
14. Fasted
17. Suffering
19. Rib
21. Reclaim
23. Trial
24. Enter
25. Lurched

**DOWN:**
1. Delve
2. Adamant
3. Obstinate
4. Desist
5. Ski
6. Bathe
7. Exerted
12. Slaughter
13. Reserve
15. Tarnish
16. Dismal
18. Facet
20. Baled
22. Air

## Puzzle 107

**ACROSS:**
7. Rabble
8. Ardent
10. Caravan
11. Genie
12. Midi
13. Aorta
17. Arias
18. Stir
22. Ashes
23. Cabaret
24. Errand
25. Eagles

**DOWN:**
1. Drachma
2. Obtrude
3. Clove
4. Frigate
5. Peony
6. Steer
9. Annoyance
14. Present
15. Startle
16. Protest
19. Camel
20. Charm
21. U-boat

## Puzzle 108

**ACROSS:**
1. Zooming
5. Bread
8. Draft
9. Unequal
10. Hag
11. Axiom
12. Ejected
14. Plasterwork
20. Astound
23. Rebus
25. Elk
26. Inexact
27. Brave
28. Thyme
29. Regress

**DOWN:**
1. Zodiac
2. Okapi
3. Isthmus
4. Gauge
5. Breve
6. Equator
7. Delude
13. Jar
15. Lottery
16. Tan
17. Workbag
18. Lariat
19. Assess
21. Usage
22. Deter
24. Blade

## Puzzle 109

| ACROSS: | DOWN: |
|---|---|
| 1. Paltry | 1. Practice |
| 7. Pioneer | 2. Ladybird |
| 8. Addition | 3. Rotor |
| 9. Covet | 4. Sin |
| 10. Tiber | 5. Angora |
| 11. Thor | 6. Veneer |
| 12. Sabre | 7. Poltergeist |
| 15. Myrrh | 9. Cosh |
| 16. Eddie | 13. Baseball |
| 19. Nave | 14. Effluent |
| 20. Swell | 15. Meat |
| 21. Crest | 17. Darwin |
| 22. Osculate | 18. Insert |
| 23. Disrupt | 20. Saucy |
| 24. Eyelet | 22. Opt |

## Puzzle 110

| ACROSS: | DOWN: |
|---|---|
| 7. Aviary | 1. Ragtime |
| 8. Loathe | 2. Pianist |
| 10. Tangent | 3. Creel |
| 11. Grime | 4. Mongrel |
| 12. Mist | 5. Attic |
| 13. Baker | 6. Sever |
| 17. Gauge | 9. Strangler |
| 18. Undo | 14. Pastime |
| 22. Alert | 15. Gnarled |
| 23. Embargo | 16. Toronto |
| 24. Stigma | 19. Lapse |
| 25. Assert | 20. Peril |
|  | 21. Abuse |

## Puzzle 111

| ACROSS: | DOWN: |
|---|---|
| 7. Looted | 1. Algebra |
| 8. Bother | 2. Nourish |
| 10. Earshot | 3. Delhi |
| 11. Lifts | 4. Goulash |
| 12. Rusk | 5. Theft |
| 13. Gloss | 6. Wrist |
| 17. Crime | 9. Stalemate |
| 18. Noun | 14. Archaic |
| 22. Perth | 15. Sojourn |
| 23. Tadpole | 16. Inferno |
| 24. Raisin | 19. Spurn |
| 25. Matron | 20. Trait |
|  | 21. Ideal |

## Puzzle 112

ACROSS:
1. Warp
5. Item
7. Abandon
8. Friesian
10. Eddy
12. Smut
14. Nautical
16. Overcast
17. Rags
18. Plea
19. Complete
22. Outstay
23. Moor
24. Slay

DOWN:
1. Waif
2. Pate
3. Hacienda
4. Odin
5. Interior
6. Many
9. Removal
11. Draught
13. Toreador
15. Ultimate
18. Palm
19. Cute
20. Lays
21. Edgy

## Puzzle 113

ACROSS:
1. Rusty
4. Observe
8. Coypu
9. Javelin
10. Tee
11. Irish
13. Courage
14. Gargle
17. Wyvern
21. Scapula
22. Rabid
24. Née
25. Stipend
26. Virus
27. Erratum
28. Lotus

DOWN:
1. Rocking
2. Styli
3. Youth
4. Object
5. Savoury
6. Release
7. Ernie
12. Sag
15. Readier
16. Loudest
18. Via
19. Nudists
20. Tandem
21. Susie
22. Revel
23. Burnt

## Puzzle 114

ACROSS:
1. Arsonist
7. Label
8. Balalaika
9. Sly
10. Epic
11. Stance
13. Marble
14. Beacon
17. Breach
18. Aria
20. Boa
22. Rhodesian
23. Rumba
24. Ethnical

DOWN:
1. Amble
2. Soldier
3. Nile
4. Stilts
5. Obese
6. Playpen
7. Launder
12. Algebra
13. Members
15. Cardiac
16. Accost
17. Balmy
19. Annul
21. Neon

## Puzzle 115

**ACROSS:**
1. Last
3. Composed
9. Bleep
10. Sangria
11. Lot
13. Crescendo
14. Clause
16. Reborn
18. Lassitude
20. Set
22. Blotter
23. Split
25. Eternity
26. Coal

**DOWN:**
1. Libel
2. Sue
4. Oyster
5. Panache
6. Strenuous
7. Dragoon
8. Epic
12. Transpose
14. Calibre
15. Smitten
17. Turret
19. Easy
21. Total
24. Leo

## Puzzle 116

**ACROSS:**
2. Chaos
4. Acclaimed
6. Status
8. Slates
10. Salty
11. Global
12. Crater
13. Sling
15. Sicily
16. Easier
18. Endurance
19. Elect

**DOWN:**
1. Scarab
2. Cactus
3. Simply
4. Avalanche
5. Determine
6. Shoes
7. Sadly
8. Stone
9. Satyr
13. Sludge
14. Garnet
17. Breeze

## Puzzle 117

**ACROSS:**
1. Lace
5. Arch
7. Dialect
8. Tenement
10. Axel
12. Stye
14. Defender
16. Democrat
17. Dais
18. Stem
19. Bulletin
22. Utensil
23. Digs
24. Solo

**DOWN:**
1. Lost
2. Edge
3. Calendar
4. Left
5. Attained
6. Hail
9. Entreat
11. Emeriti
13. Enormous
15. Fatalist
18. Sand
19. Beef
20. Eels
21. Nero

## Puzzle 118

**ACROSS:**
1. Major
4. Vendor
9. Irksome
10. Tepee
11. Eery
12. Operate
13. Pie
14. Maul
16. Trek
18. Toy
20. Panache
21. Wail
24. Otter
25. Deluded
26. Decamp
27. Water

**DOWN:**
1. Maiden
2. Joker
3. Rook
5. Entreaty
6. Deprave
7. Reeled
8. Defoe
13. Plectrum
15. Agnatic
17. Uphold
18. Teddy
19. Glider
22. Audit
23. Blow

## Puzzle 119

**ACROSS:**
1. Jolly
4. Sum
8. Inure
9. Agitate
10. Conceal
11. Doing
12. Ablaze
14. Behind
17. Arena
19. Earring
22. Epitome
23. Drill
24. Gas
25. Troll

**DOWN:**
1. Journal
2. Liege
3. Yearly
4. Spindle
5. Miami
6. Emerged
7. Disc
12. Academy
13. Zealous
15. Initial
16. Cement
18. Eying
20. Radio
21. Gala

## Puzzle 120

**ACROSS:**
1. Peak
3. Scaffold
9. Patio
10. Jingles
11. Rum
13. Telescope
14. Kettle
16. Detest
18. Subnormal
20. Sag
22. Mallard
23. Trace
25. Residues
26. Omit

**DOWN:**
1. Paper
2. Apt
4. Cajole
5. Finesse
6. Onlookers
7. Dissect
8. Boat
12. Mothballs
14. Kashmir
15. Leotard
17. Smudge
19. Lute
21. Guest
24. Aim

## Puzzle 121

ACROSS:
7. Europe
8. Sombre
10. Essence
11. Sever
12. Code
13. Weird
17. Banal
18. Axis
22. Clung
23. Cuisine
24. Friend
25. Dances

DOWN:
1. Defence
2. Crusade
3. Spend
4. Tonsure
5. Above
6. Ferry
9. Relevance
14. Tangent
15. Extinct
16. Asperse
19. Scoff
20. Tunic
21. Cigar

## Puzzle 122

ACROSS:
1. Lagos
4. Chasm
10. Lionize
11. Unfed
12. Iceni
13. Upsurge
15. Ohms
17. Beano
19. Scent
22. Up to
25. Bizarre
27. Idols
29. Comma
30. Amassed
31. Asian
32. Tense

DOWN:
2. Above
3. Opinion
5. Hauls
6. Saffron
7. Blair
8. Begum
9. Adder
14. Psst
16. Hour
18. Enzymes
20. Coinage
21. Aback
23. Pecan
24. Aside
26. Riata
28. Oasis

## Puzzle 123

ACROSS:
1. Bible
4. Skewer
9. Luggers
10. Naiad
11. Army
12. Allegro
13. Nil
14. Give
16. Noel
18. Hug
20. Finesse
21. Step
24. Ernie
25. Veranda
26. Tussle
27. Hitch

DOWN:
1. Ballad
2. Begum
3. Epee
5. Kindling
6. Wriggle
7. Red-hot
8. Usual
13. Newsreel
15. Innings
17. Effect
18. Heave
19. Splash
22. Tenet
23. Arch

## Puzzle 124

ACROSS:
1. Gnome
4. Hippy
10. Tombola
11. Nasal
12. Vista
13. Orchids
15. Gene
17. Alien
19. Atone
22. I-spy
25. Ceilidh
27. Paste
29. Frump
30. Diocese
31. Teeth
32. Snort

DOWN:
2. Names
3. Moorage
5. Ionic
6. Passion
7. Stave
8. Capon
9. Bliss
14. Reap
16. Enid
18. Leisure
20. Typhoon
21. Scoff
23. Shade
24. Fever
26. Input
28. Spear

## Puzzle 125

ACROSS:
1. Pastel
7. Updated
8. Abundant
9. Deneb
10. Eager
11. Earl
12. All in
15. Totem
16. Liner
19. Deck
20. Sidle
21. Eddie
22. Antelope
23. Ingoing
24. Garden

DOWN:
1. Peaceful
2. Sturgeon
3. Elder
4. Apt
5. Cavell
6. Yemeni
7. Undertaking
9. Dram
13. Landlord
14. Nineteen
15. Tree
17. Iodine
18. Editor
20. Siena
22. Ant

## Puzzle 126

ACROSS:
4. Feeble
5. Wart
7. Dissent
10. Rajah
11. Android
12. Vogue
14. Wrapper
15. Genie
16. Dazzled
20. Bigot
21. Elderly
22. Eden
23. Umpire

DOWN:
1. Tessa
2. Gland
3. Matador
4. Foil
6. Teacup
8. Entreat
9. Trapeze
10. Riveted
13. Devise
14. Widowed
17. Llama
18. Devil
19. Glue

## Puzzle 127

ACROSS:
1. Deputy
4. Petal
8. Miami
9. Rampage
10. Grounds
11. Rhea
12. Ebb
14. Tail
15. Echo
18. Emu
21. Etty
23. Notable
25. Mongrel
26. Otter
27. Trait
28. Street

DOWN:
1. Damage
2. Pianola
3. Triangle
4. Pomp
5. Trash
6. Leeway
7. Prose
13. Beetroot
16. Habitue
17. Hermit
19. Uncle
20. Ferret
22. Tonga
24. Grit

## Puzzle 128

ACROSS:
1. Veneer
4. Delay
8. Lapse
9. Austria
10. Erudite
11. Idol
12. Mug
14. Mesh
15. Inca
18. Toe
21. Trap
23. X-raying
25. Leather
26. Treen
27. Sitar
28. Scanty

DOWN:
1. Velvet
2. Neptune
3. Eyesight
4. Dash
5. Lurid
6. Yearly
7. Harem
13. Gigantic
16. Crimean
17. Stylus
19. Exert
20. Agency
22. Apart
24. Thor

## Puzzle 129

ACROSS:
1. Punk
5. Burr
7. Netball
8. Hostelry
10. Drey
12. Helm
14. Tendency
16. Hawthorn
17. Noun
18. Star
19. Vitality
22. Academy
23. Weal
24. Soul

DOWN:
1. Pith
2. Knot
3. Stiletto
4. Zany
5. Bludgeon
6. Ruby
9. Operant
11. Encrust
13. Maternal
15. Nineteen
18. Slew
19. Vial
20. Lays
21. Yowl

## Puzzle 130

**ACROSS:**
4. Saloon
5. Omen
7. Deviate
10. Atone
11. Rissole
12. Music
14. Emperor
15. Aroma
16. Pitcher
20. Stall
21. Earache
22. Rhyl
23. Fiance

**DOWN:**
1. Flair
2. Poets
3. Amateur
4. Suet
6. Nuncio
8. Airmail
9. Essence
10. Almoner
13. Orator
14. Employs
17. Habit
18. Rainy
19. Shoe

## Puzzle 131

**ACROSS:**
1. Satsuma
5. Miser
8. Airship
9. Swang
10. Nadir
11. Anymore
12. Eschew
14. United
17. Austere
19. Unapt
22. Ad-lib
23. Achieve
24. Endow
25. Daycare

**DOWN:**
1. Stain
2. Tired
3. Unhorse
4. Appeal
5. Misty
6. Seaport
7. Ragweed
12. Emanate
13. Castled
15. Naughty
16. Herald
18. Elbow
20. Arena
21. Theme

## Puzzle 132

**ACROSS:**
1. Zulus
4. Auditor
8. Segment
9. Copes
10. Facia
11. Spruced
13. Rota
15. Lambda
17. Raglan
20. Tsar
22. Delight
24. Types
26. Forge
27. Incisor
28. Readmit
29. Enrol

**DOWN:**
1. Zestful
2. Logic
3. Steward
4. Attest
5. Decor
6. Topical
7. Rased
12. Para
14. Oath
16. Malaria
18. Article
19. Nostril
21. Strict
22. Defer
23. Gleam
25. Poser

## Puzzle 133

**ACROSS:**
4. Dapper
5. Scam
7. Quarter
10. Wrath
11. Arrayal
12. Rears
14. Airport
15. Trout
16. Torrent
20. Mayor
21. Tetanus
22. Haul
23. Tingle

**DOWN:**
1. Opera
2. Meter
3. Scarlet
4. Daub
6. Mature
8. Traitor
9. Rampart
10. Warrant
13. Wreath
14. Autocue
17. Eerie
18. Tango
19. Dude

## Puzzle 134

**ACROSS:**
1. Venue
4. Abbess
9. Lyrical
10. Cigar
11. Suet
12. Realism
13. Rip
14. Hebe
16. Ache
18. Jet
20. Closure
21. Saga
24. Trill
25. Elegant
26. Arnica
27. Tiler

**DOWN:**
1. Valise
2. Nerve
3. Etch
5. Baccarat
6. English
7. Scrimp
8. Slurp
13. Republic
15. Erosion
17. Scotia
18. Jewel
19. Barter
22. Avail
23. Feat

## Puzzle 135

**ACROSS:**
1. Tablet
4. Angry
8. Names
9. Lumbago
10. Enigmas
11. Stye
12. Tin
14. Toll
15. Ajar
18. Ewe
21. Rich
23. Gesture
25. Approve
26. Agate
27. Exert
28. Detect

**DOWN:**
1. Tandem
2. Bambino
3. Ensemble
4. Alms
5. Grant
6. Yeomen
7. Blast
13. Nauseate
16. Adulate
17. Arcane
19. Egret
20. Defeat
22. Copse
24. Pout

## Puzzle 136

**ACROSS:**
1. Wealth
7. Removal
8. Restored
9. Askew
10. Resin
11. Agra
12. Miaow
15. Mercy
16. Ernie
19. Mega
20. Drums
21. Leapt
22. Terminal
23. Queried
24. Angler

**DOWN:**
1. Wardrobe
2. Assassin
3. Thorn
4. Wed
5. Bonsai
6. Gazebo
7. Repatriated
9. Army
13. Autumnal
14. Whistler
15. Meet
17. Rhesus
18. Impart
20. Demon
22. Tee

## Puzzle 137

**ACROSS:**
1. Termini
5. Carer
8. Liberated
9. Cad
10. Plaza
12. Natural
13. Domesticating
15. Sustain
17. Highs
19. Eli
20. All around
22. Dunce
23. Yorkers

**DOWN:**
1. Tulip
2. Rib
3. Inroads
4. Intentionally
5. Cadet
6. Recurring
7. Red flag
11. Admission
13. Descend
14. Adherer
16. Adage
18. Sides
21. Use

## Puzzle 138

**ACROSS:**
1. Abbey
3. Pancake
6. Mention
8. Leeds
10. Text message
12. Roar
13. Mimic
15. Sage
17. Scotch broth
19. Label
20. Begging
21. Seattle
22. Magma

**DOWN:**
1. Armour
2. Either
3. Pun
4. Chess
5. Easter
7. Outright
9. Pedigree
10. Tango
11. Allah
14. Psalms
15. Stigma
16. Enigma
18. Theft
20. Bee

## Puzzle 139

**ACROSS:**
2. Bud
5. Carbine
8. Tale
9. Peal
11. Ton
14. Calorie
15. Orbited
16. Add
18. Beat
20. Seek
21. Earlobe
22. Act

**DOWN:**
1. Lumbago
3. Mane
4. Snap
6. Bayonet
7. Mariner
10. Pan
11. Tea
12. Nod
13. Pea
17. Dialect
19. Tear
20. Sobs

## Puzzle 140

**ACROSS:**
1. Harold
4. Spiral
7. Thesis
9. Last
11. Era
12. Peal
13. Sailor
14. Tying
16. Disc
17. Heed
18. Incur
21. Entire
23. Trio
25. Rim
26. Drip
27. Odious
29. Teapot
30. Employ

**DOWN:**
1. Hates
2. Roe
3. Desert
4. Salami
5. Rate
6. Lapland
8. Solicitor
10. Spaghetti
15. You
16. Dentist
19. Carpet
20. Remote
22. Essay
24. Idea
28. Owl

## Puzzle 141

**ACROSS:**
7. Oxygen
8. Amidst
9. Unopened
10. Bat
11. Decadent
13. Dodo
14. Bait
16. Yodelled
18. Egg
19. Stranger
22. Asthma
23. Retain

**DOWN:**
1. Excuse
2. Ignorant
3. Knee
4. Talented
5. Fir
6. Island
12. Egyptian
13. Delegate
15. August
17. Earwig
20. Acre
21. Why

## Puzzle 142

**ACROSS:**
1. Barter
4. Ballad
8. Aisle
10. Oasis
11. Recur
12. Nanny
14. Nests
16. Art
18. Axis
19. Oath
21. Sty
24. Agent
27. Faith
29. Olive
30. Yearn
31. Tiara
32. Needle
33. Thresh

**DOWN:**
1. Brainy
2. Resin
3. Every
5. Acorn
6. Lasts
7. Desist
9. Scar
13. Nixon
15. Extra
16. Ass
17. Toy
20. Canyon
22. Tail
23. Sheath
25. Erase
26. Tonal
27. Fetch
28. Image

## Puzzle 143

**ACROSS:**
1. Fumes
4. Discard
8. Use
9. Rhyme
10. April
11. Drown
12. Verse
14. Dowry
17. Ate
19. Retain
21. Lichen
23. Dry
25. Comet
28. Arson
30. Amass
31. Ionic
32. Knave
33. Owe
34. Flatten
35. Windy

**DOWN:**
1. Forever
2. Mayor
3. Suede
4. Deport
5. Stand
6. Arrow
7. Delay
13. Shake
15. Occur
16. Rue
17. And
18. Ely
20. Ego
22. Nunnery
24. Reason
25. Chief
26. Mania
27. Tacit
28. Askew
29. Spain

## Puzzle 144

**ACROSS:**
1. Carve
4. Burglar
8. Ado
9. Never
10. Weakest
11. Dam
12. Odour
13. Actress
16. Enigma
19. Prying
24. Presume
27. Seven
28. Apt
29. Pot luck
30. Ridge
31. Emu
32. Sharper
33. Mural

**DOWN:**
1. Condone
2. Ravioli
3. Eardrum
4. Bowman
5. React
6. Liege
7. Rites
14. Ray
15. Son
17. Nor
18. Gas
20. Rostrum
21. Invader
22. Genteel
23. Beaker
24. Pipes
25. Extra
26. Usurp

## Puzzle 145

| ACROSS: | DOWN: |
|---|---|
| 1. Fault | 1. Foliage |
| 4. Sardine | 2. Unravel |
| 8. Large | 3. Their |
| 9. Resolve | 4. Screen |
| 10. Adverse | 5. Risotto |
| 11. Trout | 6. Igloo |
| 12. Enlist | 7. Eject |
| 14. Bonnet | 13. Sarcasm |
| 18. Sober | 15. Nostril |
| 20. Blossom | 16. Tombola |
| 22. Anomaly | 17. Obeyed |
| 23. Torso | 18. Stays |
| 24. Schemed | 19. Broth |
| 25. Delta | 21. Opted |

## Puzzle 146

| ACROSS: | DOWN: |
|---|---|
| 1. Cat | 1. Central |
| 3. Scale | 2. Theft |
| 8. Genie | 3. Secure |
| 9. Custard | 4. Arsenal |
| 10. Curator | 5. Exact |
| 11. Notch | 6. Width |
| 12. Palace | 7. Eggcup |
| 14. Alight | 13. Cashier |
| 18. Chess | 15. Growing |
| 20. Ravioli | 16. Trivet |
| 22. Cushion | 17. Prince |
| 23. Raise | 18. Cocoa |
| 24. Large | 19. Easel |
| 25. Sag | 21. Virus |

## Puzzle 147

| ACROSS: | DOWN: |
|---|---|
| 1. Pantry | 1. Police |
| 4. Abacus | 2. Niece |
| 8. Leeds | 3. Rusty |
| 10. Noisy | 5. Bingo |
| 11. Thing | 6. Chime |
| 12. Chewy | 7. Styles |
| 14. Obese | 9. Bias |
| 16. Asp | 13. Whole |
| 18. Hoot | 15. Brace |
| 19. Adam | 16. Ate |
| 21. Eft | 17. Pat |
| 24. Hated | 20. Chorus |
| 27. Hello | 22. Flat |
| 29. Abate | 23. Colony |
| 30. Rabbi | 25. Tuber |
| 31. Ratio | 26. Daisy |
| 32. Strays | 27. Heron |
| 33. Energy | 28. Later |

## Puzzle 148

**ACROSS:**
1. Bow
3. Class
8. Amnesia
9. Newel
10. Ochre
11. Texture
12. Racing
14. Cactus
18. Carving
20. Sober
22. Trail
23. Overtly
24. Endue
25. Son

**DOWN:**
1. Bench
2. Western
3. Chaste
4. Annex
5. Sawdust
6. Halve
7. Favour
13. Carcase
15. Abscess
16. Strays
17. Ignore
18. Catch
19. Idled
21. Baton

## Puzzle 149

**ACROSS:**
7. Eclair
8. Useful
9. Generous
10. Evil
11. Ass
13. Valentine
16. Flagstaff
19. Ebb
22. Plus
23. Wisteria
24. Behead
25. Violet

**DOWN:**
1. Access
2. Camel
3. Arrogant
4. Huss
5. Select
6. Bunion
12. Sea
14. Effusive
15. Ire
17. Lulled
18. Gasket
20. Boiler
21. Below
23. Wade

## Puzzle 150

**ACROSS:**
7. Canada
8. Exodus
9. Cardigan
10. Papa
11. Cyst
12. Resolute
14. Abattoir
17. Bare
19. Came
20. Vanquish
21. Eleven
22. Dodger

**DOWN:**
1. Canary
2. Bandit
3. Kangaroo
4. Wean
5. Gospel
6. Output
13. Serenade
15. Beadle
16. Twelve
17. Bounds
18. Rested
20. Vane

## Puzzle 151

| ACROSS: | DOWN: |
|---------|-------|
| 1. Din | 1. Deserve |
| 3. Basic | 2. Nappy |
| 8. Ale | 3. Beside |
| 9. Aesop | 4. Silence |
| 10. Sultana | 5. Chant |
| 11. Arrayed | 6. Beach |
| 12. Notch | 7. Banana |
| 14. Acetic | 13. Cue |
| 17. Better | 15. Cot |
| 21. Stamp | 16. Impress |
| 23. Evinces | 18. Tackled |
| 25. Israeli | 19. Reside |
| 26. Ailed | 20. Denial |
| 27. Apt | 21. Saint |
| 28. Easel | 22. Agree |
| 29. End | 24. Irate |

## Puzzle 152

| ACROSS: | DOWN: |
|---------|-------|
| 1. Dreary | 1. Desist |
| 4. Clothe | 2. Eclat |
| 8. Salvo | 3. Roots |
| 10. Nabob | 5. Linda |
| 11. Third | 6. Taboo |
| 12. Sates | 7. Embryo |
| 14. Agony | 9. Bier |
| 16. Art | 13. Ebony |
| 18. Boil | 15. Grime |
| 19. Acid | 16. Ale |
| 21. Ebb | 17. Tab |
| 24. Freya | 20. Affray |
| 27. Peace | 22. Back |
| 29. Incur | 23. Meteor |
| 30. Rebus | 25. Elbow |
| 31. Agree | 26. Aisle |
| 32. Yawned | 27. Prank |
| 33. Skewer | 28. Arrow |

## Puzzle 153

| ACROSS: | DOWN: |
|---------|-------|
| 1. Superb | 1. Simian |
| 4. Acacia | 2. Pasha |
| 8. Mason | 3. Rinse |
| 10. In-law | 5. China |
| 11. Stern | 6. Cello |
| 12. Agape | 7. Always |
| 14. Agony | 9. Deer |
| 16. Ire | 13. Plane |
| 18. Maim | 15. Glory |
| 19. Anon | 16. Imp |
| 21. Par | 17. Ear |
| 24. Adieu | 20. Madcap |
| 27. Tying | 22. Axle |
| 29. Balsa | 23. Egress |
| 30. Credo | 25. Ideal |
| 31. Cable | 26. U-boat |
| 32. Polite | 27. Tacit |
| 33. Stress | 28. Imbue |

## Puzzle 154

**ACROSS:**
1. Rodeo
4. Gripper
7. Seine
8. Raced
10. Cue
11. Emu
12. Dread
14. Mayor
15. Ringer
18. Values
22. Scour
23. Rhyme
26. Tea
27. Ape
28. Fresh
30. Giant
31. Absence
32. Nerve

**DOWN:**
1. Rancour
2. Dosed
3. Olive
4. Greedy
5. Pea
6. Radar
8. Rumba
9. Coypu
13. Rag
16. Noose
17. Earth
19. Lam
20. Science
21. Prague
22. Sofia
24. Yearn
25. Eater
29. See

## Puzzle 155

**ACROSS:**
1. Groove
4. Lizard
8. Among
10. Unity
11. Usher
12. Eyrie
14. Ensue
16. Jet
18. Plea
19. Each
21. Boa
24. Recto
27. Sedge
29. Theft
30. Duvet
31. Igloo
32. Escort
33. Egress

**DOWN:**
1. Gravel
2. Odour
3. Vague
5. Inure
6. Amiss
7. Dryden
9. Shoe
13. Inlet
15. Niche
16. Jab
17. Tea
20. Grudge
22. Over
23. Heroes
25. Civic
26. Otter
27. Sting
28. Delve

## Puzzle 156

**ACROSS:**
1. Idaho
3. Approve
6. Protest
8. Crumb
10. Terminology
12. Road
13. Alley
15. Tell
17. Premonition
19. Ebony
20. Adopted
21. Existed
22. Deter

**DOWN:**
1. Impair
2. Hatred
3. Act
4. Rural
5. Embryo
7. Semolina
9. Injected
10. Table
11. Often
14. Sphere
15. Topple
16. Larder
18. Minus
20. Add

## Puzzle 157

**ACROSS:**
1. Dunce
4. Edited
9. Unicorn
10. Fauna
11. Lied
12. Scalpel
13. Ash
14. Spar
16. Cute
18. Axe
20. Sell-out
21. Peel
24. Extra
25. Airline
26. Plenty
27. Motet

**DOWN:**
1. Double
2. Naive
3. Eros
5. Defiance
6. Trumpet
7. Deadly
8. Gnash
13. Arrogant
15. Palette
17. Asleep
18. Atlas
19. Albeit
22. Exist
23. Tram

## Puzzle 158

**ACROSS:**
4. Ailing
5. Term
7. Promote
10. Liszt
11. Epaulet
12. Gable
14. Illegal
15. Rhine
16. Infidel
20. Scott
21. Easiest
22. Swap
23. Thread

**DOWN:**
1. Flame
2. Anita
3. Recital
4. Awry
6. Muzzle
8. Opulent
9. Eugenie
10. Legates
13. Whacks
14. Initial
17. Dacha
18. Liven
19. Used

## Puzzle 159

**ACROSS:**
1. Wing
5. Card
7. Impeach
8. Panorama
10. Vary
12. Crib
14. Thriller
16. Tree frog
17. Year
18. Epic
19. Falsetto
22. Elastic
23. Yard
24. Howl

**DOWN:**
1. Wasp
2. Giro
3. Splatter
4. Data
5. Chivalry
6. Drey
9. Air-drop
11. Re-enact
13. Breached
15. Regulate
18. Envy
19. Flan
20. Each
21. Opal

## Puzzle 160

**ACROSS:**
7. Abseil
8. Dynamo
10. Tickled
11. April
12. Main
13. Arias
17. Slate
18. Inca
22. Adult
23. Obviate
24. Subway
25. Sinner

**DOWN:**
1. Ragtime
2. Psychic
3. Rifle
4. Pyjamas
5. Marry
6. Koala
9. Adoration
14. Flotsam
15. Uncanny
16. Madeira
19. Manse
20. Busby
21. Avail

## Puzzle 161

**ACROSS:**
1. Literary
5. Rood
8. Baritone
9. Odes
11. Booksellers
14. Lag
16. Rodeo
17. Toe
18. Spindle-legs
21. Tidy
22. Warhorse
24. Duel
25. Clarinet

**DOWN:**
1. Lobe
2. Throb
3. Retrograde
4. Run
6. Oddment
7. Disaster
10. Altogether
12. Sedge
13. Closeted
15. Griddle
19. Siren
20. Jest
23. Awl

## Puzzle 162

**ACROSS:**
7. Haunch
8. Bedlam
10. Retreat
11. Tense
12. Oval
13. Stone
17. Drama
18. Scar
22. Aisle
23. Noxious
24. Morbid
25. Wizard

**DOWN:**
1. Chariot
2. Nuptial
3. Scree
4. Destiny
5. Alone
6. Umber
9. Statement
14. Arsenic
15. Scholar
16. Crusade
19. Balmy
20. Usurp
21. Oxlip

223

## Puzzle 163

**ACROSS:**
1. Usher
4. Stave
10. Coaster
11. Taste
12. Radon
13. Vampire
15. Cool
17. Pluto
19. Telex
22. Zion
25. Sweeten
27. Cairo
29. Eland
30. Ivanhoe
31. Adorn
32. Stork

**DOWN:**
2. Scald
3. Extinct
5. Totem
6. Vestige
7. Scorn
8. Bravo
9. Vexed
14. Alto
16. Ooze
18. Leeward
20. Enchant
21. Islet
23. India
24. Doyen
26. Tudor
28. Ichor

## Puzzle 164

**ACROSS:**
7. Aviary
8. Gutter
10. Lattice
11. Zorro
12. Oxon
13. Heart
17. Fibre
18. Visa
22. Fable
23. Titanic
24. Runway
25. Wasted

**DOWN:**
1. Balloon
2. Fiction
3. Train
4. Buzzard
5. Stern
6. Troop
9. Celebrate
14. Mineral
15. Dignity
16. Cascade
19. Afire
20. T-bone
21. Straw